The Politics of AIDS

By the same author
A Year in the Death of Africa
Drops in the Ocean

PETER GILL has recently led a major campaign against Aids in India for the BBC World Service Trust. He has been a foreign correspondent for the *Daily Telegraph* in South Asia and the Middle East, and has travelled widely in the developing world as a TV reporter for Thames Television, Channel 4 and the BBC. He edited *Africa Express* for Channel 4 and he was one of the journalists who brought the 1984 Ethiopian famine to the world's attention. He then wrote a definitive account of that tragedy, *A Year in the Death of Africa*.

The Politics of AIDS

How They Turned a Disease into a Disaster

Peter Gill

Viva Books Private Limited

New Delhi • Mumbai • Chennai • Kolkata • Bangalore • Hyderabad

First Indian Edition 2007

VIVA BOOKS PRIVATE LIMITED

4737/23 Ansari Road, Daryaganj, New Delhi 110 002
E-mail: vivadelhi@vivagroupindia.net, Tel. 42242200

Plot No. 76, Service Industries, Shirvane, Sector 1, Nerul, Navi Mumbai 400 706
E-mail: vivamumbai@vivagroupindia.net, Tel. 27721273, 27721274

Jamals Fazal Chambers, 26 Greams Road, Chennai 600 006
E-mail: vivachennai@vivagroupindia.net, Tel. 28290304, 28294241

B-103, Jindal Towers, 21/1A/3 Darga Road, Kolkata 700 017
E-mail: vivakolkata@vivagroupindia.net, Tel. 22836381, 22816713

7, Sovereign Park Apartments, 56-58, K. R. Road, Basavanagudi, Bangalore 560 004
E-mail: vivabangalore@vivagroupindia.net, Tel.26607409, 26607410

101-102 Mughal Marc Apartments, 3-4-637 to 641, Narayanguda, Hyderabad 500 029
E-mail: vivahyderabad@vivagroupindia.net, Tel. 27564481, 27564482

Published by arrangement with

Profile Books Ltd.
3A Exmouth House, Pine Street
London ECIR OJH
UK

ISBN 81-309-0414-4

Published by Vinod Vasishtha for Viva Books Private Limited, 4737/23 Ansari Road, Daryaganj, New Delhi 110 002. Printed & bound by Raj Press, R-3 Inderpuri, New Delhi.

Contents

A Death in Zambia

Esther Kamusa, divorced and the mother of a little girl, was 37 when she died. It happened on a morning in June 2005, at the Mothers of Mercy Hospice at Chilanga, a township on the broad highway that sweeps south from Lusaka towards Zambia's border with Zimbabwe.

Locals used to call the hospice 'the place of the black gate'. Sister Stanisława Smarzoch from Poland thought that sounded too funereal and had the big double doors repainted yellow, brown and green. The doors now also bear the words 'Welcome to the Hospice' in bold white lettering.

Esther had arrived at the hospice four weeks earlier, her immune system fatally compromised by HIV, the Human Immunodeficiency Virus, which without treatment leads to Aids. She was already seriously ill with tuberculosis. Worse than that, she was bitter about the life she had lived and the death that awaited her. She railed against the faithless husband who had infected her and then run off with another woman. She was worried about her daughter back in the village and upset that she would not see her home again. 'There is no God,' this Zambian Christian told Sister Stanislawa.

In fact Esther Kamusa found peace of mind in her final days. When proper food, clean water and medicine made her a little stronger, Sister Stanislawa arranged for her to be driven home for a final visit and to say a gentle goodbye to her 7-year-old daughter.

As pneumonia began to suffuse her lungs, Esther appeared even to regain some of her faith. Sister Stanislawa would read the Bible to her. 'At the end, she was the one who was doing the praying,' she said, 'and it was she who said "God is the one who created me. Whatever happens now, it is His will." '

By the evening of 24 June, heavier and heavier doses of antibiotics were failing to hold back the tide of infection in Esther's body. When Sister Stanislawa got up from her bedside that night and said she was going to sleep, she thought Esther might already have slipped into unconsciousness. But Esther raised a frail arm in salutation.

I arrived at those newly painted gates at 10 a.m. on 25 June. The Chilanga Hospice is the product of a generous private Dutch donation and has twenty beds. That morning only the tiny four-bed children's ward had a vacancy. The men's and women's wards, each containing eight beds, were full with the very sick and the dying. I spoke to those who could manage a conversation and noticed the little knot of women around one bed in the female ward, speaking softly to the shrunken figure lying in it.

Sister Stanislawa took me to her office, a hut in the middle of the hospice compound, to tell me about the state of Aids around her. The Mothers of Mercy have been organizing volunteers for home visits in the parish since the early 1990s. As the epidemic intensified during that last appalling decade of the twentieth century, they found that the sick were simply being dumped on their doorstep by desperate families too poor to cope. Sometimes the dying would be left propped up against a tree or slumped in a wheelbarrow in the hope that good Samaritans would come along and take care of them. That was why the Chilanga Hospice came into being.

Aids is getting worse, Sister Stanislawa told me. She had no doubt about that. The drugs that the Zambian government and the rich world now promise are certainly a help, but they are not yet widely available and not all of them are free. For the dirt poor of St Mary's parish around Chilanga, five pounds a month for medicine is a fortune. Sometimes the families of the sick scrape together enough money to start a course of drugs, but there is no cure for Aids and treatment lasts a lifetime. Then they run out of money, often even for the minibus ride to the clinic. They stop taking the drugs and their immune system rapidly collapses. 'They get very sick and they die,' she said. 'It's shocking.'

She spoke about all the other work the Mothers of Mercy do in the parish and the school they run for 130 poor and orphaned children, more than 100 of them with HIV. Chilanga may be only ten miles from the country's capital and on a major highway, but still only 12 of those 100 or so children are on Aids drugs, and those only through private charitable sponsorship. Then there are all the other things that Sister Stanislawa needs, from fuel for the vehicle to a blood test machine. 'The problem is we have no regular income,' she says, and she places her two hands palm-upwards on the office table. 'We have to keep asking everyone with outstretched arms.'

As we stepped out of her office, I noticed two women sitting on the hospice steps, their heads resting on their knees, sobbing. They were Esther's sisters. Esther Kamusa had died at 11.15 a.m. on 25 June 2005. Sister Stanislawa cried too.

The parish of St Mary's is divided into eight zones. On the day of my visit, there was a meeting of the women who lead the teams of volunteers for the Aids home visits in each of those zones. Since it was a Saturday, they were meeting in one of the school classrooms, decorated by the children with paintings of things which they aspired one day to own, mainly shoes and bicycles.

Sister Stanislawa and I had interrupted their meeting, and so I was invited to talk to the volunteer leaders. They were among the African women on whom the impact of the Aids epidemic has fallen so disproportionately. Not only are they in danger of being infected by their men – many more women than men are falling ill with Aids – they must also bear the burden of caring for sick relatives, feeding their families and bringing up their children in poverty.

I told them I was a journalist, and I asked each in turn to single out her biggest problem in trying to help her community deal with Aids. Two of the eight mentioned a lack of food and clean water. But all of them kept coming back to their one great need – transport. Not the four-wheel drive transport of the aid agencies, but the simple village transport of a bicycle, and access to local public transport. How can you get a sick person from the village to the main road, they asked, if you do not have a bicycle on which to push him? How can you get a sick person to the hospital – or a patient to the clinic to pick up his drugs – if you do not have a pound for the bus fare, or two pounds if he is so sick he needs to be accompanied? I had no answers to those questions, other than to acknowledge the blindingly obvious – that poverty is at the heart of Africa's Aids crisis.

I left Chilanga Hospice at about 1 p.m. As I drove out through those painted gates, Esther's body was being wheeled on a trolley from the female ward round the corner to the hospice morgue.

Esther Kamusa was one of 2.4 million who died of Aids in sub-Saharan Africa in 2005, and one of the estimated 25 million who have died worldwide since the epidemic was first recognized in the United States in 1981 – a million for each year of the epidemic. At the time of Esther's death, there were almost 26 million Africans infected with the Aids virus, two-thirds of the world total of 40 million.

The figures are mind-numbing, and no one visiting Zambia can be in any doubt as to the enormity of the Aids catastrophe – the sheer number living with the virus in poor residential districts; the schools, hospitals and offices understaffed through sickness; the unexplained deaths, often of quite prominent people, recorded in the newspapers; and all the casual conversations that lead back to the individual tragedies of Aids.

Nor is Zambia, where roughly one in six adults has the virus, the worst affected country in southern Africa. In South Africa about one in five adults has the virus; in Zimbabwe it is one in four; in Lesotho it is more than one in four; in Botswana and Swaziland it is more than one in three.

As the twenty-fifth anniversary of the global Aids epidemic approached in 2006, the world was showing signs of finally responding to this immense crisis. The World Health Organization of the UN declared that there should be 3 million people on Aids treatment by the end of 2005. WHO does not itself command great resources and has failed by a long way to reach this figure, but at least it has had the boldness to set a target in the first place.

Under George W. Bush, the United States passed legislation promising to put 2 million people in fifteen poor countries on Aids drugs by the end of his second term in 2008. It also undertook to prevent 7 million new infections. With $15 billion earmarked for this initiative, it was the largest ever commitment by any country to combating a disease. Other countries and agencies made corresponding pledges. World leaders promised to aim for universal access to Aids treatment by 2010.

These belated undertakings raise questions that this book seeks to answer. What were governments and other global institutions doing in the first quarter-century of the Aids pandemic? How responsible are they for the body count of 25 million and the 40 million who are living compromised lives because of the Aids virus? Did Esther Kamusa have to die at the age of 37 in that hospice outside Lusaka?

There is another, more critical question. Is the world, under American leadership, responding any more effectively to Aids in the twenty-first century than it did in the last century? How many more Esthers will die and how many more children will be left without parents because of Aids?

1

Sex and Sin

'Everything about this epidemic has been utterly predictable, utterly, utterly, utterly and completely predictable ...'

Dr Mathilde Krim, Aids specialist, New York, 1987

At the age of 70, Larry Kramer is still a very angry man. You hear that anger as you listen to him talking about the early years of Aids in New York and the numbers who are sick today in America and around the world. He is disheartened at having said the same thing over and over again for twenty-five years. He now believes the war on Aids has been lost, and that it was lost in the actions and inactions of American officials in the 1980s.

Larry Kramer is a playwright, novelist, film producer and coruscating journalist. An article entitled '1,112 and Counting', published in the *New York Native* in 1983, ranks as perhaps the single most telling piece of journalism in the history of Aids. It was aimed at New York gays and began: 'If this article doesn't scare the shit out of you, we're in real trouble. If this article doesn't rouse you to anger, fury, rage and action, gay men have no future on this earth. Our continued existence depends on just how angry you can get.'

Right at the beginning of the epidemic, in 1981, Kramer co-founded Gay Men's Health Crisis, still going strong, and then went on to establish ACT UP which brought startling public protest to bear on American indifference to Aids.

Kramer is gay. He was diagnosed HIV-positive in 1987 and has recently had a liver transplant. He survives on a cocktail of powerful drugs, and frequently feels rotten.

I wanted to meet him, but he wasn't very keen to see me. He said he was 'interviewed-out' and everything he needed to say was in his latest book, *The Tragedy of Today's Gays*. I tried again, by email, and said that one of the things I wanted to discuss was the level of official culpability for the Aids death toll.

As well as being angry, Larry Kramer can also be rude. He wrote back (all in lower case): 'every single person who has died has died because of official negligence. this is now a very naïve question to be asking and indicates to me how much you have yet to learn ... I have no doubt that aids is a plague that has been intentionally allowed to happen and to continue. This is no longer crazy talk. the facts support it.'

After that, we met at his apartment in Lower Manhattan. He was just getting over a heavy cold, which I then caught. His condemnation of the early American response to Aids is mirrored by his sense of pessimism about the present. The drugs that keep him and so many others alive do not, he said, represent much of an improvement.

'I question the use of the word improvement, simply because so many more people are sick. No, I don't think there's been an improvement. I think it's got grotesquely worse. It's very unclear where the treatments which appear quite useful are going to take us. I look upon them as a house of cards that could come tumbling down the longer we take them.'

Kramer has no more time for the administration of George W. Bush than he had for his Republican predecessor Ronald Reagan who presided over the early years of Aids. When I spoke about the generosity of the new American response to Aids in the poor world, and the moral obligation America had undertaken to continue to provide drugs for Africa, he shot back: 'You think they care? I'm sure they'll find many excuses to say people don't qualify.' Then he raised his voice to a shout: 'You don't understand. They don't give a shit and nobody is holding their feet to the fire.'

The American and then the global Aids crisis began with a report of a cluster of rare pneumonias among gay men, published in the medical bulletin *Morbidity and Mortality Weekly Report* on 5 June 1981. Because of the homosexual connection, that first report was played down, just as most other early reports of the epidemic were played down, even in the city where the impact was worst. *The New York Times*, a particular target for the anger of Kramer and the early activists, managed just three reports in 1981 and three more in 1982, all of them on inside pages.

In those early years Kramer made speeches and wrote articles condemning Congress for failing to fund Aids work, federal health officials for not authorizing more research and, most vehemently of all, city officials in New York for not responding to this enormous crisis within its large homosexual community. Fellow Aids activists believed Kramer wildly overstepped the mark in his early assaults on Mayor Ed Koch who ran the city from 1978 to 1989. But Kramer did not moderate his personal criticisms then, nor does he do so now. In his latest book *The Tragedy of Today's Gays*, published in 2005, he wrote: 'Of all the people in the world I condemn Koch as the person most responsible for allowing HIV to grow unimpeded from 41 cases to the more than

70 million now being tallied. It was on his watch it all began. He could have sounded the first and most important alarm; to the city, to the President, to the media, to the world. In any and every way he did not do so.'

Ronald Reagan was in his early months as President when the epidemic started and it famously took him six years to utter the word 'Aids' in public. When he did speak, to the American Foundation for Aids Research in May 1987, Larry Kramer was there to boo him in person.

Reagan's first speech was about the merits of mandatory testing for Aids, but he was thrown a shouted question as he boarded the presidential jet afterwards. 'What should people do about Aids?' 'Just say no,' was the presidential answer. By the middle of 1987, when the President gave that advice, more than 25,000 Americans had died of the disease and a further 30,000 had been infected.

It was not just the activists who argued that it could all have been different. On the platform with the President that evening was Dr Mathilde Krim, co-chair of the Aids research foundation and a leading specialist in the disease. It was then, and not with the benefit of a further twenty years' hindsight, that she declared: 'Everything about this epidemic has been utterly predictable, utterly, utterly, utterly and completely predictable, from the very beginning, from the very first day. But no one would listen. There are many people who knew exactly what was happening, what would happen and has happened, but no one of importance would listen. They still won't listen. This is an epidemic that could have been contained. We definitely could have contained it.'

So why was Aids allowed to rage out of control in New York and other major American cities? It is not easy for public officials in any political culture to talk openly about sex. But twenty-five years of the Aids epidemic have laid down one hard and fast rule – those nations that overcame political squeamishness and confronted the realities of Aids have managed, more or less, to contain it. The obverse is also true – those countries, like America, that failed to react swiftly and publicly have developed significant epidemics.

What is true of public officials around the world and of heterosexual sex is even truer of homosexuality. Aids, after all, was initially the 'Gay Plague'. The Reagan era was also the era of 'The Moral Majority' and witnessed the emergence of the religious right as a political force. For an influential American constituency, Aids was not primarily a public health emergency. It was the Wages of Sin.

First came the right-wing commentator Patrick Buchanan, a former speech-writer for President Nixon. As Aids took hold in New York, San Francisco and elsewhere, he pronounced: 'The sexual revolution has begun to devour its children ... The poor homosexuals – they have declared war upon nature, and now nature is exacting an awful retribution.'

It was left to preachers to bring down the wrath of God. 'What gays do to each other', said the Reverend Jerry Falwell's *Moral Majority Report*, 'makes them sick and, more and more frequently, dead!' He offered this Old Testament judgement: 'Aids is a lethal judgement of God on the sin of homosexuality and it is also the judgement of God on America for endorsing this vulgar, perverted, and reprobate lifestyle ... God destroyed Sodom and Gomorrah primarily because of the sin of homosexuality. Today, He is again bringing judgement against this wicked practice through Aids.'

Where the commentators and the Christian preachers led, the political right followed. 'Every Aids case can be traced back to a homosexual act,' said Senator Jesse Helms. The only real way to deal with the threat to America's health was to 'slam the door on the wayward, wanton sexual revolution which has ravaged this nation'.

Many years later, as we shall see, Senator Helms underwent something of a conversion to the cause of Aids relief, but in 1987 he slammed the door by introducing a measure in Congress banning any organization that advocated or promoted homosexuality from receiving government funds. For four years, before it was successfully challenged in the courts, this measure meant that gay organizations were unable to use federal money to relay important Aids prevention messages.

'Hundreds of thousands of Americans were probably infected with HIV between 1988 and 1992,' says the American writer Peter Lewis Allen in his book *The Wages of Sin: Sex and Disease, Past and Present*. 'Could effective education have prevented 10 per cent of these infections? 5 per cent? Even if only one infection in a hundred could have been averted, the cost of sparing the country's moral sensibilities ranked in the thousands of lives.'

In the ostrich-like denial of the Reagan administration, there was one exception. Dr C. Everett Koop was sworn in as United States Surgeon General in November 1981 after months of bitter resistance from the Democrats in Congress. One congressman dismissed him as 'Dr Kook'. The Democrats thought they were reviewing the credentials of a right-wing ideologue, but he turned out to be a disappointment to his own backers. To the consternation of the Reagan White House, Dr Koop became one of the first public health heroes to emerge from the global Aids disaster.

What recommended Dr Koop to Ronald Reagan's team was his fierce opposition to abortion. A few years before the Reagan victory he had co-authored a book and presented a documentary on the subject called *Whatever Happened to the Human Race?* In one scene in the documentary, Dr Koop stood on the shore of the Dead Sea, where hundreds of little dolls had been artfully placed to float in the background, and declared: 'Sodom comes easily to mind when one contemplates the evils of abortion and the death of moral law.' Dr Koop was a committed Christian, tall, angular and bearded. Everyone said that he actually *looked* like an Old Testament prophet.

What the White House had failed to appreciate, however, was that Dr Koop's pro-life stance on abortion would simply be applied to the developing Aids crisis. 'I realized that if ever there was a disease made for a Surgeon General, it was Aids,' Koop observed in his memoirs, adding: 'If ever there was a public in need of education and straight talk about Aids, it was the American people.'

In his ninetieth year in 2005, Dr Koop was still making his contribution to American public health from the C. Everett Koop Institute at Dartmouth College, New Hampshire. He told me that in 1981, as an innocent in the ways of government, he had naïvely failed to gain concrete guarantees from the White House that he would be able to do his duty in each and every public health area, including Aids. Instead, just as Reagan remained silent, so too for five long years did the White House impose its silence on the Surgeon General.

'Whenever I spoke on a health issue at a press conference or on a network morning TV show, the government public affairs people told the media in advance that I would not answer questions on Aids, and I was not to be asked questions on the subject.'

He broke his silence finally, and appropriately, in an interview with *Christianity Today*. By then he calculated he had given more than 200 official addresses on health issues 'before I ever addressed any segment of the American public on the most mysterious and most vexing health issue of the century'.

Koop's next step was to prepare a report on the Aids epidemic which was published, after twenty-seven drafts, in October 1986. It underscored the importance of abstinence and monogamy, but it also dealt with homosexuality, and the need for sex education in schools and for condom promotion. 'I used the terrible word "condom," ' he recalled, 'and that was probably the most serious word that I used in my entire tenure as Surgeon General.'

White House officials were furious about the report's explicitness, and demanded revisions. Koop had written: 'Most Americans are opposed to homosexuality, promiscuity of any kind and prostitution.' They wanted it changed to 'All Americans are opposed …' 'I could not say it because it was not true,' Koop retorted. Within a few weeks of publication the White House suggested a second edition to 'update' Dr Koop's findings. The 'update' they had in mind was to drop all references to condoms. The Surgeon General refused.

White House objections to the report were mild compared with the reaction from the right wing in the country. An outspoken activist, Phyllis Schlafly, was outraged at Koop's recommendation that sex education needed to start early in schools and accused him of promoting 'safe sodomy and safe fornication'. The admirable Koop was beyond intimidation. 'I'm not Surgeon General to make Phyllis Schlafly happy. I'm Surgeon General to save lives.'

Koop encountered wilder views even than those of Phyllis Schlafly. He recalled discussing a proposal for Aids screening with a California Congressman, William Dannemeyer. He asked the Congressman what he would do if it was possible to identify every HIV-positive person in the country. 'Wipe them off the face of the earth,' was the reply.

The battles Koop fought led to more and more people learning about Aids and how to prevent it. In 1988 the US government finally authorized the posting of a six-page flyer entitled 'Understanding Aids: A Message from the Surgeon General' to 107 million households. It was the largest mailing in United States history. It happened seven years after the epidemic was first identified and well over a year after a number of other Western countries, with far less developed and far smaller epidemics, had done the same.

There is a pointed cartoon of the era from the *Boston Globe* showing President Reagan saying to an aide: 'Not doing enough? What are they talking about? Didn't Koop just mail the whole country his filthy little book?'

On the issue that divides America today and, through American influence, helps divide many nations most affected by Aids, Dr Koop says: 'If you have people who don't listen to the good public health messages they hear, to the good moral messages they hear, then the only thing left is the condom. I could not in good conscience exclude anything that saves lives. I was the Surgeon General of the United States, not the chaplain of the United States. It was not easy for a person of my age [he was 65 when appointed], a husband, father and grandfather, to become known as the "Condom King". I held no brief for condoms, but my message was that the moralist and the public health official could walk down the same path.'

After the years of denial under Ronald Reagan, the presidency of the first George Bush had one remarkable consequence for people with HIV around the world. They were essentially banned from travelling to the United States. HIV had been placed on a list of diseases that merited exclusion in the final months of the Reagan administration, but the ban was enforced during the Bush presidency.

It is possible in some circumstances for HIV-positive people to enter America, but they must first apply for an HIV visa waiver. That opens them to questioning and searches on arrival in the US and can complicate other international travel. Many HIV-positive people choose not to go at all or, for fear of intrusive searches, travel without disclosing their status, sometimes sending their anti-HIV drugs on ahead by post.

As a result of the travel ban, the big biennial international Aids conference was switched from Boston to Amsterdam in 1992, and the organizers have never brought it back to the United States. Bill Clinton campaigned for the lifting of the ban when he was running for president and still says it should be reviewed, but he ducked the opportunity to do so when in office.

Since leaving office, Bill Clinton's travels to the developing world and the work of the Clinton Foundation on HIV/Aids have underlined his reputation as a great communicator. His Aids initiative has successfully negotiated money-saving deals with drugs manufacturers and medical suppliers for the benefit of poor countries. 'I really believe this is the worthiest thing I could have done as the main initiative of the administration at this point in history,' he told a reporter from *New York* magazine in Zanzibar in the summer of 2005. Then he corrected himself. 'Not administration, Foundation.'

Bill Clinton began his presidency by giving prominence to Aids in his inaugural address in January 1993. 'The world economy, the world environment, the world Aids crisis, the world arms race – they affect us all.' But what did he actually do during his years as President when Aids spread around the globe and threatened catastrophe in Africa?

Clinton's senior Aids official for most of his second term was Sandy Thurman, a former head of Aids Atlanta, in Georgia. She very nearly didn't take the White House job because she was so unimpressed with the lack of commitment to Aids during the first Clinton term. Once in the job, she was determined to try and get real resources devoted to Aids in the poor world.

Apart from the funding challenges, there was a series of policy decisions taken during the Clinton presidency that undermined the quality and vigour of the US response to Aids, at home and abroad. For a start the ban on HIV-positive visitors to the United States was signed into law again in 1993. On the emblematic issue of drugs prices and treatment for people in the poor world, it was only in the final months of his presidency and after a sustained and rowdy protest campaign that Clinton finally reversed White House support for the pharmaceutical companies in their battle against the South African government, which I describe in Chapter 5.

But Clinton's worst political funk was over how to respond to the transmission of HIV through intravenous drug use. Dirty needles are an even more deadly and efficient way of transmitting the virus than sex. By 1998 there had been a ban for nine years on any federal funding of needle-exchange programmes. It was a highly contentious political issue, but the administration said it was committed to lifting the ban provided the science justified it.

The National Institutes of Health, the government's top medical body, backed by other scientific institutions, declared the ban to be seriously compromising efforts to tackle Aids. Dr Anthony Fauci, the top Aids expert at the National Institutes who reviewed all the epidemiological evidence, said to me: 'We came to the conclusion that needle-exchange programmes had a positive and beneficial effect in regard to HIV. There didn't seem to be a significant increase in the use of illicit drugs. So the recommendation I made was "Go with needle exchange." They asked for the recommendation and I gave it. But it didn't get clearance from the White House.'

President Clinton changed his mind at the eleventh hour, swayed apparently by political calculations and the opposition of General Barry McCaffrey, his senior anti-drugs official. The two men had travelled together to South America the weekend before the scheduled announcement of a lifting of the ban on needle-exchange programmes. Plans for a Monday morning press conference had to be abruptly scaled down and plans for the big announcement scrapped. For Sandy Thurman, Clinton's senior Aids official, this was 'my biggest battle and my biggest loss. The fact of the matter is that the science was so weak on their side and so strong on ours. The press conference was all set up and then off the President goes with Barry McCaffrey, and Barry convinces him that this is the wrong thing to do. It was a political decision. It was not a decision based on science, and we lost. Bill Clinton is a political creature more than anything else, and Barry is very convincing.'

Right at the end of the Clinton presidency, Sandy Thurman fought a final funding battle for international Aids. She had already gained substantial increases. What had begun as a commitment of tens of millions of dollars a year at the start of the Clinton presidency had now risen to several hundred million a year. 'We did a lot and I'm proud of what we did. But at the end we did not give the people on the ground what they needed to do their work.' Her last request was cut back by two-thirds. 'They choked and didn't give us what we needed.'

By the time Bill Clinton left office after the 2000 presidential election, the US annual commitment to global Aids had crept up to $350 million. Within two years, George W. Bush had committed his administration to a five-year programme of

$15 billion, representing a nine-fold increase on the Clinton expenditure.

Sandy Thurman offered an ironic and shocking judgement on the failure of the Clinton administration to do more. She believes it was that failure which provided a political opportunity for his successor. 'If we had been more successful, George Bush would never have taken Aids up. If there had been a serious Clinton initiative on Aids, George Bush and his advisers would never have touched it.'

2

God and Abstinence

'Abstinence takes on Hollywood.
Lights, Camera, No Action.'
Abstinence Clearinghouse slogan, 2005

The latest *Star Wars* film is subtitled *Revenge of the Sith*. Senator Tom Coburn adapted the title to 'Revenge of the STDs' – Sexually Transmitted Diseases – for a scary sex talk he gave in one of the big basement rooms on Capitol Hill in May 2005. His staff said it was aimed at helping young congressional workers living in pressure-cooker Washington, but they made sure that the press was invited as well. Horror film music introduced the Senator's hour-long slide show about all the unpleasant things that disease can do to the human sex organs.

Tom Coburn is a doctor from Oklahoma, as well as a Republican and a Christian. 'I will try not to give an opinion,' he began. 'My patients find that when I give them the information, they modify their behaviour patterns.' The information that Dr Coburn passed on was that there was an epidemic of sexually transmitted diseases raging in America; that where fifty years ago there were 'only two known sexually transmitted diseases' there were now more than twenty-five; and that two-thirds of all STD cases occur among young people under the age of 25.

'What would happen if young women under 20 started saying no to sex?' he asked as he looked around the room. 'Disease would be down, pregnancies would be down and you'd all get a rest.'

Aids ranks as a persistent public health crisis in America. At the end of 2003, more than 1 million Americans were living with HIV or Aids. In New York City, the figure crept for the first time above 1 per cent of the population. In the country as a whole, Aids affects African Americans most seriously, accounting for more than half of all cases. Black women between the ages of 25 and 44 are thirteen times more likely to die of the disease than their white counterparts.

Dr Coburn, recently elected to the US Senate, started giving his sex talks to young staffers when he was still a Congressman. They never excited quite as much interest as the one I attended in 2005. Sex and what to do about it had by then become one of the most divisive issues in American politics, one of the defining domestic clashes of the Bush era. Senator Coburn was a key figure among the abstainers and had played a decisive role in shifting American policy both at home and abroad from condom to abstinence promotion.

In 2005 it was almost as if the US Congress was running a 'Summer of Abstinence' on Capitol Hill. A few days before Senator Coburn's talk, I attended another packed meeting there. This time the invitation was issued by Democrats. This was a 'research briefing'. Dr Hannah Bruckner, from Yale University, was there to present the findings of a study following the lives of young Americans who had taken virginity pledges as part of the 'True Love Waits' programme in the early 1990s. By 1995 more than 2 million young people – 12 per cent of all adolescents – had taken the pledge. But what happened next?

Some of what the study found was music to the ears of the abstinence promoters. Dr Bruckner found that those who had taken the pledge started having sex later than those who did not. Pledgers were likely to have had fewer sex partners as well as fewer partners at the same time, and they also got married earlier. Exactly the sort of result 'True Love Waits' had been hoping for.

But this was not the whole story. 'We were expecting to find lower STD rates,' she said. In fact, the researchers found no significant difference between those who had taken the pledge and those who had not. The reason for this, said Dr Bruckner, was that most of the young people taking the pledge ended up having premarital sex anyway, even if later and with fewer partners. When they did so, they were less likely to use condoms and less likely to go for check-ups or treatment. The shame and embarrassment at failing to keep the pledge put them at greater risk of getting infected. 'My projection', said Dr Bruckner, 'is that the negative effect of not using condoms would negate the advantage of delayed sexual intercourse.'

Balanced scientific judgements like Dr Bruckner's have not informed the current American debate. Sexual conduct and the system of sex education intended to influence it are now one of America's great divides. Abstainers battle it out with the proponents of comprehensive sex education. Accusations of 'junk science' are traded by both sides and both offer 'evidence-based' defences. First sex may be delayed by abstinence-only campaigning in the schools, but it does not appear to have a long-term impact on the sex lives of young Americans, still less on the risks they face of infection.

As the abstainers gleefully point out, some of the earliest federal grants for domestic abstinence programmes were authorized by President Bill Clinton. But it is since the election of George W.

Bush that funding has taken off. From $80 million in 2001, it had more than doubled by 2005. President Bush promised that it would almost treble to $270 million by the end of his second term. In the first five years of the Bush presidency, the United States spent an estimated $1 billion on abstinence campaign programmes.

The purpose of these programmes is to encourage US schoolchildren to abstain from sex until marriage. Federal rules lay down that these programmes should teach 'abstinence from sexual activity outside marriage as the expected standard for all school age children' and that 'a mutually faithful monogamous relationship in the context of marriage is the expected standard of human sexual activity'. Schoolchildren must learn, say these rules, that 'sexual activity outside the context of marriage is likely to have harmful psychological and physical effects' and that it is important to attain 'self-sufficiency before engaging in sexual activity'.

This means that there is little or no room for condoms or safe sex messages. One federal programme specifies that schools using abstinence funds 'must agree not to provide a participating adolescent [with] any other education regarding sexual conduct in the same setting'. In other words, condoms are not to be discussed in schools taking federal abstinence funds. In the late 1980s, only 1 school in 50 in America held abstinence-only classes. By 2005 a third of all schools did so, accounting for about 8 million schoolchildren.

When the organization Human Rights Watch was preparing its 'Ignorance Only' report on abstinence-only programmes in 2002, it chose to study the state of Texas where George W. Bush had been Governor. One teacher, from Laredo, Texas, summed up the approach: 'We don't talk about HIV/Aids prevention except to say, "Remain abstinent until marriage and once married, be monogamous with your spouse." We don't talk about contraception or condoms because that would be crossing the line that the state or federal guidelines have set. We don't mention the word "condoms" at all. If a student brings it up, he's directed to speak with other people, like his parents or a counsellor.'

America's leading public health institutions have had to make adjustments to the politics of abstinence. At the beginning of 2002, there was a condom fact sheet on the website of the Centers for Disease Control which read: 'The correct and consistent use of latex condoms during sexual intercourse – vaginal, anal, or oral – can greatly reduce a person's risk of acquiring or transmitting most STDs, including HIV infection.' The fact sheet was then removed and a 'Being Revised' message was substituted.

It was later replaced with this: 'The surest way to avoid transmission of sexually transmitted diseases is to abstain from sexual intercourse or to be in a long-term mutually monogamous relationship. For persons whose sexual behaviors place them at risk from STDs, correct and consistent condom use of the male latex condom can reduce the rate of STD transmission. However, no protective method is 100 per cent effective, and condom use cannot guarantee absolute protection.'

Those behind the abstinence movement are aiming at a counter-revolution in America, a chance to reverse thirty years or more of sexual liberalism and to start repairing the damage, as they see it, done by the first sexual revolution.

The Heritage Foundation has been a key promoter of the abstinence revolution at home and abroad. This influential conservative think-tank says it was the issue of welfare dependency that first triggered its interest in the 1990s when it argued that problems like teenage pregnancy, youngsters on benefit, and family breakdown could all be addressed with stronger abstinence education in schools.

'We're talking about behavioural expectations here,' said Jennifer Marshall, the foundation's director of domestic policy. 'Are you going to have an abstinence expectation or an expectation of promiscuity? We do not necessarily have a problem with basic education about condoms. What we support is that that component should be taught separately – as part of a health pack, as part of a biology class, but not as part of the abstinence curriculum.'

Jennifer Marshall's colleague Melissa Pardue, responsible for some of the Heritage Foundation's many reports on the merits of abstinence, added another justification for this focus. 'Abstinence education is character regeneration,' she said. 'There's been condom promotion for thirty-five years. Under their watch all we've had is sky-rocketing teen pregnancies and STD rates.'

Outside Washington, there have been some remarkable outriders for the abstinence movement. Leslee Unruh, president and founder of Abstinence Clearinghouse, has her home and headquarters in Sioux Falls, South Dakota, but flies in regularly to do business in the capital.

The day I met Mrs Unruh had begun for her with a meeting in the West Wing of the White House with Claude Allen, one of the President's top domestic policy advisers. Abstinence Clearinghouse received a $3 million grant from the US government for its role in training teachers and monitoring the new abstinence-only school curricula. 'They have to understand what this law lays down if they are getting federal dollars,' she told me.

To say that Mrs Unruh is a determined advocate of abstinence does not do her justice. She has no time for condoms, at all.

'Are we going to continue with this terrible lie that latex is the answer?' she demanded.

'Isn't latex part of the answer?' I asked.

'No, it is causing more grief. Condoms don't protect, obviously, so we see high suicide rates and depression.'

'Would you reduce condom promotion further?'

'I would teach abstinence and faithfulness, exclusively. I would not be promoting condoms.'

Mrs Unruh started an 'unwed mothers' home' in Sioux Falls in the 1980s. She had counselled young women through her husband's anti-abortion work and the crisis pregnancy centre they ran together. She told me she had been raped when she was a girl and that her husband had been her only consensual sex partner. She has five children, four of them married. All four were virgins until marriage, she said. The two girls removed their 'purity rings' at their weddings and handed them to their father, who passed them in turn to their new husbands. 'I am giving you the most precious gift I have,' they said. 'I'm giving you the gift of my virginity.'

One of the girls had not even kissed her husband before the wedding, said Mrs Unruh. 'We practise what we preach.' And then: 'Abstinence is taking the world by storm and Europe is just about five years behind us.' When I met Mrs Unruh she was preparing for the ninth Abstinence Clearinghouse conference, to be held in Los Angeles. 'Abstinence takes on Hollywood,' said the flyer. 'Lights, Camera, No Action.' Mrs Unruh told me she also had plans for extending the work of Abstinence Clearinghouse to Africa.

Ranged against the abstinence campaigners are the lobbyists who argue for a comprehensive approach to sex education, including safe sex and condom promotion. The weapons of war between these two camps are the reports they conduct into each other's programmes. Academic researchers find themselves in the middle

– or more often co-opted by one side or the other.

In one of its assaults on safe sex education, the Heritage Foundation mocked 'The Wonderful World of Condoms' and singled out a programme called 'Be Proud! Be Responsible!' which advises students to shop for condoms with their sexual partners: 'Buy lots of different brands and colours. Plan a special day when you can experiment. Just talking about how you'll use all those condoms can be a turn-on.'

Safe sex proponents hit back with their own examples. The leading lobby group is the Sexuality Information and Education Council of the United States which tore into an abstinence-only school curriculum promoted by an organization called 'Choosing the Best'. The programme advised teachers to bring a rose into class, talk about how beautiful it was, and then pass it round the class, telling each student to pull off a petal until there were none left. 'Ask: Of what value is the rose now? Share that the rose represents someone who participates in casual sex. Each time a sexually active person gives that most personal part of himself or herself away, that person can lose a sense of personal value and worth.'

The Sexuality Information and Education Council complained that abstinence curricula produce distorted information on condoms. This is what 'Choosing the Best' said about them: 'Couples who use condoms for birth control experience a first-year failure rate of about 15% in preventing pregnancies. This means that over a period of five years, there could be a 50% chance or higher of getting pregnant with condoms used as a birth control method.' Wrong, said the council. Students needed to know that 'when used consistently and correctly, condoms are 98% effective in preventing pregnancy and research has shown that using a condom for HIV prevention is 10,000 times safer than not.'

Argument here revolved around 'method failure' and 'user failure'. Abstainers have blamed pregnancies on condom failure even when they were not used consistently as a birth control method. The condoms did not fail; couples simply failed to use them the whole time.

At the Washington office of the Sexuality Information and Education Council, Bill Smith is Vice President in charge of public policy. On the day we met, the newspapers were full of a story from the suburbs where conservative parents had formed a group called 'Citizens for a Responsible Curriculum' and forced the local school board to abandon its new sex education curriculum. The curriculum had allowed some discussion of homosexuality, including the assertion that being gay was 'not a mental disorder', and had also included an instructional video about condom use.

'It is very clear that abstinence-only-until-marriage is on the cusp of undermining our entire success in this country on HIV prevention,' Bill Smith said. 'It is a huge lie for this administration to say that HIV prevention hasn't worked and that we need a new strategy. That is not true. We have levelled off infections to about 40,000 a year. We know that the more comprehensive and condom-centred programmes have been the key to educating the average population and reducing the numbers. Teenagers on abstinence-only programmes are less likely to use contraception and they're more likely to get STDs. Half of all new HIV infections are among young people. Why? Because they are not learning about condoms and contraception in school.'

The virtues of abstinence have been a regular theme in the presidential addresses of George W. Bush. He even has a little joke with which he rounds off his homilies on the subject, and which he repeats with some frequency. Apparently aware that the research cannot always be relied upon to back him on the advantages of abstinence-only education, he said in 2002: 'You know, I've heard all the talk about the abstinence programmes, and this that and the other, but let me just be perfectly plain. If you're worried about teenage pregnancy, or if you're worried about sexually transmitted disease, abstinence works every single time.'

It was under Bush's direction that America's sexual counter-revolution was first exported. What was good for young people in America would be good for young people – and adults – in the Aids-affected countries of Africa.

To begin with, George Bush was not much moved by the plight of Africa. Domestic matters took precedence in the 2000 presidential campaign. Early on in the race, he told a television interviewer: 'While Africa may be important, it doesn't fit into the national strategic interests, as far as I can see them.' Twenty words – that was it. In one of the set-piece TV debates just before the election, Bush was asked specifically about humanitarian intervention in the continent. 'Africa is important,' he reiterated, 'but there's got to be priorities.'

What happened to turn such disengagement into the largest and most radical intervention on global Aids ever mounted appears to have been a change of heart within that critical Bush constituency, the evangelical Christians. In particular, the Reverend Franklin Graham, son of the Reverend Billy Graham, became convinced through the African work of his missionary organization Samaritan's Purse that it was an overriding Christian duty to respond to the Aids disaster.

In February 2002 Franklin Graham organized an 'international Christian conference on HIV/Aids' in Washington called 'Prescription for Hope'. More than 800 Protestants, Roman Catholics and others came together to 'equip the Church to respond biblically to Aids'. It was no surprise that a number of senior Washington politicians and some of the administration's top aid officials also attended the conference. Some had links with Mr Graham's missionary organization, but there was also an important family connection. It was Franklin Graham's father who had prompted the first steps that George W. Bush took in the 1980s from heavy-drinking hell-raiser to born-again Christian.

Among the politicians who heard harrowing accounts of the African Aids disaster that day was Senator Jesse Helms, the man who had so vehemently objected to a proper response at home because of the connection between Aids and homosexuals. 'I'm so ashamed I've done so little,' he told this gathering. 'I will do better than I have done in the past and I will work together with you.' A month later, in an article in the *Washington Post* entitled 'We Cannot Turn Away', Helms proposed a new US commitment of $500 million to tackle mother-to-child Aids transmission. 'In the end, our conscience is answerable to God. Perhaps, in my eighty-first year, I am too mindful of soon meeting Him, but I know, like the Samaritan travelling from Jerusalem to Jericho, we cannot turn away when we see our fellow man in need.'

Mothers and children were the so-called 'innocent victims' of Aids. Their plight did not have to unsettle harsh notions of sin and sinners. Others with Aids would not as easily be folded into Helms's Christian embrace. In 2005, now 84 and retired from the Senate, he recalled in his memoirs: 'It had been my feeling that Aids was a disease largely spread by reckless and voluntary sexual and drug-abusing behavior, and that it would probably be confined to those in high-risk populations. I was wrong.' He was not, of course, saying that he was wrong in his condemnation of all those reckless, voluntary and drug-abusing sinners.

Franklin Graham himself seemed to have travelled rather

further than Mr Helms in his response to Aids. During the Washington conference he gave an interview to *USA Today* and was asked what the big obstacles were to greater church engagement in the Aids issue. 'The biggest is conservative Christians, although I don't point my finger just at conservatives,' he replied. 'Certain people would say that this is God's judgement. But I as a Christian have to ask: What would Jesus Christ do? If Jesus were on this earth today – walking as he did 2,000 years ago – I think you would find him on the forefront of this issue, showing love and compassion.'

When asked whether he sensed any change in the attitude of Protestant evangelicals towards people with Aids, regardless of how they got sick, he replied, 'No, I don't think so, not yet. But I'm late to this issue. So I have to point the finger at myself ... I hope that in the months and years to come we will see a measurable difference. I don't see that right now.' Twenty years into the American epidemic and after almost 500,000 deaths, it was a remarkable assessment of the limits to Christian charity.

When I spoke to Franklin Graham in 2005, he told me that it was the churches, and apparently only the churches, that had the answer to global Aids. 'For me the church of Jesus Christ is on the forefront of this fight, actually facing it. In my opinion, if there's any hope, it's going to come through the churches.' The churches would educate and warn people of the perils of sex outside marriage, and they had a powerful ally in the President. 'Now George Bush is a man who has spiritual faith, and he believes the Bible and he feels that abstinence and faithfulness are what need to be taught,' he said.

The Bush White House worked on the detail of its response to global Aids through 2002, and in his State of the Union speech in January 2003 George Bush unveiled his Emergency Plan for

Aids Relief. There would now be a tripling of the present US commitment which already represented more than a doubling of the Clinton administration's spending. Bush called his plan 'a work of mercy beyond all current international efforts to help the people of Africa'. Before Iraq, before Hurricane Katrina, this would be 'can-do' America in action.

As the legislation to put Bush's promise into force sped through Congress in 2003, the true radicalism of the measure became apparent. For the first time it gave concrete, governmental expression to activists' demands that people with HIV around the world, wherever they lived and however poor, were entitled to free treatment. In an aid and development world notoriously untroubled by deadlines and the need for urgency, the President's plans also laid down specific targets. By the time he left office, the new programme would put 2 million people on treatment; it would prevent 7 million new HIV infections; and it would provide care to 10 million people sick or living with the effects of HIV and Aids, including orphans and children.

The Bush plan for Aids overseas also gave formal expression to two key strands in conservative domestic thinking – the need to allocate a big role to Christian organizations and the importance of promoting an abstinence-only-until-marriage strategy. For thirty and more years, the US had been heavily promoting condoms around the world, first for birth control when international anxiety centred on the population explosion, then to limit the spread of Aids. That emphasis would now be challenged and reversed.

What drafters and supporters of the Bush Aids legislation needed was evidence that a conservative US approach to sexual morality and disease prevention had immediate relevance for

Africa. They found it in Uganda. Then they needed academic backing for this view. They found that in the work of a Harvard social scientist and his book *Rethinking Aids Prevention*.

Dr Edward C. Green is an anthropologist by background. His CV on the Harvard website refers to his work in Aids policy reform and 'getting the United States to adopt the Uganda model of prevention'. It adds that 'his congressional testimony has been credited with being a primary resource for passage and wording of global Aids legislation and amendments (2003) and the specific development of $15 billion plan of implementation (2004)'. Redirecting the whole US approach to global Aids is a tall claim for a single academic to make, but it appears to be wholly justified.

In an email to Dr Green, I asked if he had ever reflected on the experience of influencing US policy so decisively. He replied: 'Yes, I have reflected on my personal experience. There was a precise moment in early 2001 when I declared a jihad against the billion dollar Aids industry ... the first thing I did after declaring the jihad was to write a book proposal for *Rethinking Aids Prevention*.'

Dr Green's book was published in 2003 and set out to demonstrate that Uganda's success in bringing down its HIV infection rates from 21 per cent to 6 per cent in the 1990s had everything to do with abstinence and fidelity and very little to do with condoms. This was Uganda's 'ABC' approach where A stood for Abstain, B stood for Be Faithful, and C stood for Condoms, apparently in that order. The obstacle to more effective Aids prevention in Africa, Dr Green argued, lay in an unmerited Western bias in favour of condoms. If donors were to begin to promote abstinence or fidelity, he wrote, 'and this caught on, they would stand to make no profits. This is unlikely to happen any time soon.'

'ABC' were the initials that would now drive the new American approach to African Aids. The Bush strategy document, published in early 2004, said that abstinence was to be the goal for people up to marriage, and fidelity thereafter. 'Correct and consistent condom use' was recommended only 'for those who practice high-risk behaviors'. High-risk groups were defined as 'prostitutes, sexually active discordant couples [couples where one partner is infected with HIV and the other is not], substance abusers and others'. The general population would receive 'a clear message that the best means of preventing HIV/Aids is to avoid risk all together'.

In the allocation of funds for fighting Aids around the world, the US Congress also made sure that abstinence programmes would get a big slice of the cake. Of the $15 billion promised over five years, $3 billion was to be spent on prevention and of that figure at least $1 billion dollars – a third of all prevention funds – had to go on abstinence-only-until-marriage programmes.

One month before the 2004 election which saw George W. Bush returned to the White House, the United States Agency for International Development (USAID) issued a press release detailing the first substantial grants for Aids prevention work: $100 million was being committed exclusively to abstinence-only programmes, the release said. It even repeated Mr Bush's observation about abstinence being the only certain way to avoid contracting HIV. 'It works every time.' The $100 million was to be shared between eleven organizations. Nine of the eleven were Christian. They included the Reverend Franklin Graham's Samaritan's Purse which received around $11 million to be spent on abstinence programmes in Africa.

3

The Heart of the Matter

'We are being told that only a thin piece of rubber stands between us and the death of our continent.'

President Yoweri Museveni

South of the Equator in Uganda the red earth and deep green vegetation give way to flat savannah where boys graze cattle with long and graceful horns. This is the road to Rakai and the border with Tanzania where, through scattered trees, you can glimpse the waters of Lake Victoria. This African idyll was shattered in 1978 when, in his last act of murderous folly, the dictator Idi Amin invaded his neighbour.

Rakai was also the fertile territory in which Uganda's Aids epidemic, the first to be acknowledged in Africa and for many years its worst, took root. In the economic dislocation of the Amin years, the lakeside communities became cross-border smuggling centres, and where smugglers with wads of banknotes led, the prostitutes followed. Amin's invasion of Tanzania and the counter-attack that followed accounted for the rapid spread of the disease – through rape, through prostitution, through all the profligate sex that accompanies war.

People had almost no understanding of what was happening and why they were getting ill and dying. For want of a better word, they first called the disease 'Slim' because of the way its victims simply wasted away. Locals attributed the sickness to Tanzanian witchcraft or, when the Tanzanian army finally took off after Amin, to army shellfire spreading the germs.

The chaos Amin left behind him pitched Uganda into seven more years of strife and bloodshed. Aids invaded every corner of the country, but Ugandans knew where it had started. Well into the 1990s buses arriving in Kampala from the south would be met with whistles and jeers, 'Here comes Aids, here comes Aids.'

In all its distress, Uganda has been blessed with gifted and dedicated public health officials who have stuck the course over more than two decades. Dr David Serwadda, now director of the Makerere Institute of Public Health, was one of the first researchers to identify Aids in Uganda, and is still a key figure in continuing research in Rakai.

In the early 1980s Dr Serwadda was a young medical officer at the Uganda Cancer Institute treating, among other things, a rare cancer called Kaposi's Sarcoma. 'We kept hearing about Kaposi's Sarcoma among white homosexual men, but it was also the tenth most common tumour here. There were four patients at one stage, all from the south, and they were going downhill very rapidly.'

This was the time when Aids tests first became available. All four patients from the south tested positive. 'I remember getting excited and then depressed,' said Dr Serwadda. 'Excited that we had identified the disease here, depressed at the implications.'

After Aids had been identified, documented and reported, Dr Serwadda and his colleagues applied for American funds to conduct further research in Rakai. The application was turned down. 'Then I was told to spin it a little in terms of condom use,' said Dr Serwadda. 'At that time USAID were very interested in promoting condom use as a means of preventing infection.' That was in 1985. Twenty years on, all the spinning would be in the opposite direction.

Uganda's greatest advantage in its Aids crisis was the guerrilla leader who emerged from the bush in January 1986 to take over the country. For many years Yoweri Museveni qualified as one of Africa's best post-independence leaders, progressive and forthright. I first met him in 1979 on a helicopter tour of his native south-west when he was defence minister in a post-Amin government. He wanted to talk all night about the state of Africa and the world.

During his time in the bush Museveni had followed BBC radio reports about the advance of Aids, and he began telling villagers as well as his own commanders about the new danger. Shortly after taking power he sent a group of sixty officers to Cuba for military training, and at a leaders' gathering in Zimbabwe he was taken aside by Fidel Castro who said: 'You know you've got a big problem in your country.' Castro told him that 18 of the 60 officers, 30 per cent, had tested HIV positive.

In Africa as elsewhere, it is an unvarying rule that political leaders must overcome their squeamishness and speak up loud and often about the reality of Aids. If they do not, their people suffer and die. Museveni was one of the very few leaders in Africa to do his duty. It could have been a soldier's worldliness – his own troops were a big part of the problem – and there was certainly no tourist industry to defend at that time, but Museveni shaped Uganda's response to Aids with persistence and imagination. Hundreds of thousands owe their lives to him.

One of the best accounts of Uganda's early response to Aids

comes from Dr Sam Okware, another of the country's committed public health experts. Dr Okware now runs community health programmes at the Ministry of Health, but for four years after Museveni came to power he headed the country's national Aids programme. He had begun by investigating this mysterious sickness in Rakai in the early 1980s, but he told me he did not at first connect it with events in the United States: 'We have no homosexuals here.' I let the remark pass.

Having established that Aids was also a heterosexual disease, Sam Okware went to work alongside his President on Uganda's new Aids prevention committee. This was the body that came up with the health messages that would one day so impress American officials. 'Love Carefully,' suggested Dr Okware. No, said Museveni, 'Love Faithfully.' In getting Ugandans to limit the number of people with whom they had sex, Okware considered the homespun 'Feeding in Your Own Paddock'; it was Museveni who coined the phrase 'Zero Grazing'.

The nation was being called to arms to deal with Aids. Every morning at 6 a.m., Dr Okware arranged for the beating of the national drums of war on Radio Uganda. 'Come, there's a war on! Come, we are at war!' Then there would be Aids prevention messages. They were aimed, Dr Okware told me, 'at people who had spent the night in the wrong bed'.

From the start there was an issue with condoms, as much practical as moral. Museveni did his sums and told Okware that there were enough condoms in the country to provide only four per adult male per year. That was not going to stop the Aids epidemic. There was also, the President said, a problem with mixing messages if people were told first not to be promiscuous and then advised to use condoms.

'Do you know how people do sex in the country?' asked the

former guerrilla commander. 'No, sir,' said Okware, and he got a lecture on the lack of light, on the damage done by storing condoms in hut roofs and on how men would try and use the same condom all night.

The President of Uganda's views on condoms have become a big factor in the African Aids debate. He has changed his tune more than once. In a 1991 speech, he said: 'We are being told that only a thin piece of rubber stands between us and the death of our continent. I feel that condoms have a role to play as a means of protection, especially in couples who are HIV-positive, but they cannot be the main means of stemming the tide of Aids ...' Then he made the crucial practical point: 'In countries like ours, where a mother often has to walk twenty miles to get aspirin for her sick child or five miles to get water at all, the question of getting a constant supply of condoms may never be resolved.'

At an international conference in 2004, Museveni attacked 'those who want to "condomise" the world by telling us that it holds the ultimatum solution', but when I was in Uganda researching this book in 2005 he gave a gathering of East African Roman Catholic bishops a different message: 'If the Church is really interested in seeing its followers live, it should back the use of condoms to save its own people from Aids. I am not trying to support immorality by supporting those who cannot abstain and be faithful to use condoms, but there is a need to recognize the weakness of those we are living with and therefore help them to live.'

Museveni may be in two minds about condoms, but there is no doubting the dramatic increase in their availability in Uganda in the earlier years of the Aids crisis. In the decade to 2001, the number of subsidized 'social-marketed' condoms sold rose from 300,000 a year to 20 million. In the five years to 2001, total condom distribution grew from 4 million to 120 million a year.

Uganda's own public health experts insist that condoms played an important part in tackling the epidemic. Dr Okware points to the dramatic decline in new HIV infections in towns and cities in the early 1990s, a decline that was followed four years later by a reduction in infections in the countryside. The difference can only be accounted for, he believes, by the way in which condoms were promoted and distributed, first in urban and then in rural areas.

This was Uganda's ABC strategy in action – A for Abstinence (encouraging young people to delay having sex), B for Being Faithful (persuading adults to limit the number of their sexual partners) and C for Condoms for those who could not or would not do either A or B. It accounted for the biggest success against Aids so far seen in Africa. HIV prevalence peaked at around 20 per cent, one in five of the adult population, in the early 1990s, with some big towns recording a 30 per cent prevalence, or one in three of the adult population. In some age groups it fell to as low as 5 per cent in 2001, although figures released in May 2005 put the national prevalence rate at 7 per cent.

Dr Okware says that Ugandans are entitled to learn about all the possible individual responses to Aids, and not to have their minds made up for them. 'I don't want to be guilty of killing someone because I have withheld information or a particular intervention from them,' he told me. 'Let all the interventions go to all the people, and let them take the final decision.'

The recent troubling rise in Uganda's HIV prevalence rate suggests that partisan adherence to any one part of the ABC strategy – or indeed to the ABC strategy as a whole – may be an inadequate response to the epidemic. The 2005 figures show that HIV prevalence is lowest among 15–19 year-olds, at 3.2 per cent among girls and 1.2 per cent among boys. Ugandan youngsters are also delaying their first sexual intercourse to an average age of 18 for girls and 19 for men, a reduction of up to a year over the position in 2001. They appear, in other words, to have got the message.

But among adults in their thirties the prevalence figures have risen to 10 per cent of the population. More than two in five Ugandan marriages are 'discordant', where one partner is HIV positive and the other is negative. Women and young girls remain disproportionately at risk from infection because their sexual and reproductive lives continue to be controlled by men. Poverty forces girls to have sex with older men. Is ABC an answer for them, still less a strategy that emphasizes A and B?

Ambitious American plans for reversing the spread of global Aids began to unfold in Uganda in 2004. Each United States embassy in the countries chosen for the Bush programme was given its own targets. By 2008 in Uganda, for instance, American money would put 70,000 HIV-positive Ugandans on anti-Aids drugs, give care to 325,000 more and prevent 165,000 new infections. In 2005 the United States committed $128 million to fighting Aids in Uganda. In 2006 it was to be $185 million. Uganda is receiving more per head than any other country from the Bush programme.

The lion's share of American funds is to be spent on providing drugs for people who are already HIV-positive. It is an impressive programme, and the target of 70,000 was comfortably exceeded by 2006. In Kampala I spent a morning at the city's main hospital where The Aids Support Organization known as TASO runs clinics for HIV-positive people. TASO is the oldest voluntary Aids organization in Africa. It was founded soon after Yoweri Museveni came to power and owes much of its success to the openness and determination with which Aids was tackled in those early years.

For most of its existence TASO was able to test people for HIV, counsel them about the implications and then treat some of the infections which overwhelm people with compromised immune systems. What they could not do was keep these people alive. In the developed world a cocktail of anti-Aids drugs has been saving and extending lives since the mid-1990s, but not in the poor world. Thanks largely to the Bush programme, that has now changed.

For TASO and its clients, this is a miracle. From the end of 2004 clinic staff began working through the 30,000 HIV-positive people who had registered over the years but whose lives they could neither prolong nor save. For more than half of those on the register, it was already too late. They had sickened and died through lack of anti-Aids treatment. However, survivors were recalled for tests to confirm their HIV-positive status and to establish whether they yet needed to be put on antiretroviral drugs.

At the TASO clinic I sat for a time with a group of women and a lone man as they were told about the new treatment programme. It is the women on whom the burden of Aids falls so heavily, but it is also the women who show so much more sense in seeking help. Some in the group still seemed healthy; others had the glazed eyes and the dull, taut skin of the sickly. The counsellors took them through the advantages and the disadvantages of the treatment. It would 'help stop the virus from multiplying', it would 'help make you better', it would 'improve your appetite'. What were the bad things? 'After taking the drugs, men don't want to put on condoms.' Two of the women said their partners refused either to get tested for HIV or to use condoms.

This provision of Aids treatment is belated recognition of a human right. But it is not the answer to Africa's Aids catastrophe. These drugs are drugs for life. The more people who are treated, the more expensive it becomes. The more who become HIV positive, the more treatment will be needed. For every badly affected country in the world, this will rapidly break the bank. The frightening calculation for Uganda is that spending on anti-Aids drugs could rise to $1 billion a year. All the Aids experts are agreed – proper preventive measures are still the key.

Alongside American dollars to fight Aids in Uganda came the American debate over how to prevent sexually transmitted diseases. This imported cultural conflict served both to amplify local divisions and to jeopardize Uganda's capacity for effective Aids prevention. As in America, the discussion lent more heavily on notions of Christian order than on public health priorities. And as in America, Uganda's new brand of churchman enjoyed exceptional political access and influence.

The Reverend Martin Ssempa was brought up as a Roman Catholic but found his calling as a Baptist. He lost a brother and a sister to Aids, and he credits his own survival to seeing the light just in time. At the height of the Ugandan Aids crisis he wrote a play called *The Church and the Virus* and took it round the country with a Baptist drama group. It told the story of how becoming a Christian had saved his life. Later he met and married a New Yorker called Tracey, also a Baptist, and studied at a bible university in America, which accounts for a detectable American drawl. As a teenager, he was also the break-dance champion of East Africa, and remains an engaging showman.

I first encountered Martin Ssempa at a full-day meeting in Kampala devoted to abstinence and fidelity as the best approaches to Aids. Condoms were mentioned, but mostly to be denigrated.

This was a workshop organized by the 'Office of the First Lady of Uganda' and was described as promoting 'behavioural change on a biblical basis'. Mrs Janet Museveni, wife of the President, is a born-again Christian, and has become the country's most powerful voice in favour of abstinence for the young. Her influence extends all the way to Washington.

Mr Ssempa gave the main presentation at the workshop. He said that condoms were acceptable for married couples but should not be promoted to the rest of the population. Like others there, he complained about how difficult it was to get United States funding for abstinence programmes. 'I am getting tired of saying I'm waiting for George Bush's money,' he said. Despite US interest in funding religious organizations, there are tough financial requirements and strict rules against proselytizing with US federal money. 'Don't take PEPFAR [the President's Emergency Plan for Aids Relief] money and use it to speak about Jesus,' Martin Ssempa advised the abstinence and fidelity workshop. 'That'll be a big problem.'

Mr Ssempa runs a community church at Makerere University in Kampala where he also founded his Campus Alliance to Wipe Out Aids. On Saturday nights during term-time he takes over the university's outdoor pool area for a rock and rap show advertising the dangers of Aids and the need for abstinence. The bands have names like 'Pure Souls' and 'G3U', standing for God with Us.

In April 2005 Mr Ssempa went to Washington and took his fight to the condom promoters of America. He had been invited to give evidence to the International Relations Committee of the House of Representatives and he began by accusing the United States aid agency USAID and the official US health agency, the Centers for Disease Control, of continuing 'to promote promiscuity and condoms' and 'not allowing faith-based organizations to help us'. He said there was a new enemy in Africa's fight against Aids. 'That enemy is the Western belief that condoms can end the HIV/Aids epidemic.'

Echoing Dr Edward Green's *Rethinking Aids Prevention* which did so much to shape the congressional approach to Aids in Africa, Mr Ssempa questioned why US agencies concentrated their resources on the subsidized marketing of condoms. 'I believe it's because the Uganda ABC programme was established by Africans for Africans,' he said. 'This angers many so-called "professionals" in the Aids community who have promoted social marketing. Aids prevention is now a billion-dollar industry based upon supplying HIV prevention programmes that centre on the distribution of condoms.'

Dr Green's view is similar. In his book he wrote that 'it is glaringly clear to me that Aids prevention programmes designed by western experts have been to a large extent incompatible with the cultures of Africa and other resource-poor parts of the world'. He said the process of providing condoms and other medical products for Aids prevention in Africa 'reflects ethnocentrism and technological arrogance'. Dr Green is one of a group guiding Janet Museveni on how best to uphold Uganda's 'ABC' approach to Aids. Mr Ssempa is part of the same group.

Uganda's First Lady has been welcomed and listened to with respect whenever she travels to Washington. Her interventions in the US debate over how to respond to African Aids began when the Bush legislation was first being discussed in 2003. She wrote to Senator Richard Lugar, chairman of the Senate Foreign Relations Committee, to note 'that one of the approaches to prevention is now being referred to as the "Ugandan ABC model", namely, "Abstain, Be Faithful, Use Condoms," in that order of preference,' adding: 'We have seen it work in Uganda and I would strongly advocate that it be considered as the method that, in the long run, is likely to be the most beneficial.'

On a visit to Washington in June 2004, just as abundant US funds began to flow in Uganda, Mrs Museveni was invited to address the Medical Institute of Sexual Health. This time she declared flatly that 'condom use, as a preferred method of prevention or reduction of infection, is definitely not in the interest of Ugandans', and went on: 'Giving young people condoms is tantamount to giving them a licence to go out and be promiscuous; it leads to certain death.' Many public health campaigners insist that there is no persuasive evidence anywhere in the world that condom promotion leads to promiscuity. The evidence, they say, points the other way – the more young people know about the risks of sexual infection and the means of protecting themselves, the more responsible they will be in their sexual conduct.

When Mr Ssempa gave his testimony on Capitol Hill, he had one particular target in mind, the American non-profit organization Population Services International. PSI has impressive programmes throughout the developing world in the health, family-planning and Aids fields. In Uganda, PSI became a major player in combating Aids as the supplier of 'socially marketed' condoms where a combination of commercial advertising and subsidized prices drove sales and availability dramatically upwards.

As the mood swung in Washington from the merits of condoms to the virtues of abstinence, PSI in Kampala tried to adjust to the new political reality. The agency even got $300,000 from US funds to work on abstinence and fidelity campaigning. But the knives were now out for PSI, both in Washington and in Kampala.

'A condom social marketing firm to be a primary abstinence provider!' Mr Ssempa exclaimed to Congress. 'What a joke this would be if there were not lives at stake! How can the leading condom social marketing agency become an abstinence advocate overnight?'

The row between Mr Ssempa and PSI developed over an educational comic for teenagers called *Kikosi* (*The Gang*) on which PSI had spent some of its abstinence money. The first issues were an effective assault on the stigma which young HIV-positive people are likely to encounter, but they contained very few abstinence messages. In fact references to PSI's socially marketed 'Protector' condoms predominated. Even the prize for which readers were invited to compete was a 'Protector' T-shirt and cap. Mr Ssempa counted up all the references and sent his findings off to the office of Mrs Janet Museveni, along with an angry account of how *Kikosi* had been launched at a Kampala secondary school.

No one would tell me what exactly happened next, but there were well-founded reports in Kampala in 2005 that Mrs Museveni had directed angry accusations of 'pornography' at PSI and had suggested that the agency's future in Uganda might not be secure. So in fact it turned out.

The immediate consequence of the row was that the teenage magazine was scrapped after a few issues and undistributed copies were burned. The balance of the $300,000 that PSI had been given was redistributed to a number of Ugandan 'faith-based' organizations, including Mrs Museveni's Uganda Youth Forum. There was to be no more promotion of 'Protector' condoms either on billboards or on radio. Uganda had now come into line with the Bush plan for Aids prevention – that condoms were appropriate for high-risk groups like prostitutes, soldiers, lorry drivers and 'discordant' couples, but they were not to be promoted to the general public, still less to the young and unmarried. Abstinence and fidelity ruled.

Janet Museveni's attachment to the A and B of the ABC message has a religious and moral foundation. In a speech to young Ugandans recorded by the BBC World Service and broadcast in November 2005, she equated sex with a condom with killing and theft. 'The message that is being put before you is literally to say that if you feel like having sex, go ahead and do it as long as you use a condom. By the same token, we can also say to you that if someone makes you angry and if you feel like killing them, go ahead and kill them, or if your friend has money and you do not, go ahead and steal it.' She was then asked by the reporter if she linked morality and HIV. 'Absolutely yes, I think so, because I believe in God. He gives us a way that we should live our lives. And if we don't live by His word, we find ourselves in trouble.'

'So God punishes people for immoral behaviour with this virus?'

'Yes, I think so.'

What began as a debate in America and Uganda over the role of condoms in Aids prevention had by late 2004 in Uganda become a scandal. In October Uganda's National Drug Authority issued a public notice recalling all its 'Engabu' ('Shield') condoms and halting further distribution. 'Engabu' was the imported government brand available free of charge to the poor at health centres throughout the country. It was the most widely available condom in the country with a distribution of 60 million a year, about half the country's consumption. The result of the recall was a critical shortage of condoms throughout 2005. Prices for those still in the marketplace went up three times or more, and the poor had to do without.

Several generations of Ugandans had got used to the condom – a not very high-tech piece of Western technology – in the family planning drives of the 1970s and 1980s and then as protection against disease in the era of Aids. Ugandans had been further assured that if their own government could not provide them, an army of foreign donors would do so. In 2005 they were cruelly let down. This was not the 'can-do' philosophy in action; this was 'let them abstain' indifference. I have a pile of Ugandan newspaper cuttings from early 2005 recording increasingly anxious appeals from around the country for condom supplies. Worse was the news I heard in Kampala that refugees in the camps of the north were using plastic rubbish bags as sheaths.

I searched in Kampala for evidence that the First Lady or her allies were directly responsible for creating this crisis. I did not find it. The recall of condoms was made in response to an apparently genuine scare story about a batch that was defective, the probable result of poor storage. But condom opponents were happy to play up the problem, and the system put in place to check future supplies led to further disgraceful delays. Condoms would now have to be tested after as well as before they were shipped to the country. Since Uganda has neither manufacturing nor testing capacity, this meant that once the condoms had arrived in Uganda, samples had to be sent all the way back to Europe or America for a further round of quality testing.

The United States remains the world's largest condom supplier, and was one of the donors who eventually scrambled in 2005 to fill the condom gap left by the Ugandan government's actions. But increases in supply did not ward off fierce criticism of the American role. Stephen Lewis, the Canadian politician and former diplomat who is the United Nations Secretary-General's special envoy for HIV/Aids in Africa, said in August 2005 that the condom crisis was being 'driven and exacerbated by ... the extreme policies of the United States, resulting in great damage and undoubtedly causing a great number of infections'.

Relations between Population Services International and the First Lady of Uganda's office improved for a while after the clashes over the publication of *Kikosi*. They even worked together making advertisements about abstinence. On the airport road into Kampala, visitors to Uganda in the summer of 2005 were greeted with a huge hoarding showing a homely looking woman and the words 'She's keeping herself for marriage ... what about you?' Three organizations came together to produce this concept – PSI, USAID and the Office of the First Lady.

Congressional critics of PSI in Washington would be harder to pacify. For the religious right, PSI embodied all the excesses of an era of sexual liberalism now past. Critics pointed out that the organization was founded by Philip Harvey who runs America's biggest mail-order and online sex aids and pornography empire.

Mr Harvey started out as a student in public health working on ways to use modern marketing techniques to promote family planning, notably condoms through the post. That grew into the Adam & Eve sex business which he successfully defended through the 1980s from Department of Justice raids and obscenity prosecutions. Harvey used the profits of his sex business to fund condom and other contraceptive services in the Third World through PSI and another organization, DKT. He has been neatly described as a 'hard-core philanthropist'. But when the *Washington Times* ran an article in 2003 headlined 'USAID contracts go to porn purveyor', Mr Harvey was pressed to resign from the PSI board. His departure did not spare the organization from assault.

Senator Tom Coburn, whom we last met lecturing young congressional staff on Capitol Hill about sexually transmitted diseases, launched the fiercest attack on PSI. In May 2005 he wrote to President Bush to complain about the way US Aids funds were being spent by PSI on a project in Central America which he characterized as 'prostitute parties'. In fact the programme was a responsible effort to encourage illiterate sex workers to take care of their own health and to protect themselves from Aids.

'The project which has been funding these prostitute parties is up for renewal, and PSI has applied for tens of millions more to continue the project,' Mr Coburn wrote. 'There is something seriously askew at USAID when the agency's response to a dehumanising and abusive practice that exploits women and young girls is parties and games.'

Within two months of this complaint, USAID cancelled the renewal process and recast the application rules. PSI feared it would be knocked out of the bidding, but the press was now on to the story, other Senate opinion was mobilized and the project survived. It was not so fortunate in Uganda. In June 2005, PSI was one of the bidders for a $30 million contract to continue its work in the field of health, family planning and Aids. In August it was informed that its bid had failed.

When I met Randall Tobias, the former pharmaceutical company chief executive who served as head of the Bush Aids programme until 2006, I asked him about PSI's failure to have its contract renewed. He replied: 'There are a number of organizations who have not demonstrated a willingness to follow the ABC approach. There are people out there who believe that condoms are the answer, so it's possible that somebody didn't get a contract renewal because there was competition better able to implement the AB part of the ABC programme.'

As the old guard of liberal-minded aid institutions came under assault in the funding battles of Washington, new troops were moving in. The most telling promotion was that of a small organization called Children's Aids Fund founded and run by Anita Smith, co-chair of President Bush's advisory council on HIV/Aids, and her husband Shepherd Smith. Mr Smith introduced Senator Coburn at the congressional sex talk I attended as 'the most principled legislator I have ever had the honour of knowing'.

In 2004 the Children's Aids Fund applied for money to promote abstinence in Uganda. Its application was judged by USAID as 'not suitable for funding' and as having 'outstanding technical issues', according to documents acquired by the Democrat Congressman Henry Waxman. When the first big abstinence grants were announced in October 2004 and $100 million went to eleven organizations, Children's Aids Fund was not among them. Yet just three days before the presidential election and without a public announcement, Children's Aids Fund received its grant after all.

In a letter to Mr Tobias in February 2005, Congressman Waxman complained that the grant raised 'questions of political cronyism' and 'serious concerns about the integrity' of the grant process. I spoke to Shepherd Smith at the Children's Aids Fund, and he dismissed these concerns as a 'non-issue', explaining that his organization had simply been next on the list to receive funds for abstinence campaigning in Africa and that USAID had found, after all, that it had enough money to make another award.

Despite some embarrassment among senior US officials over this decision, the final endorsement of the Children's Aids Fund grant was made by Mr Tobias and I asked him why. He replied: 'This is a programme that is a joint venture with the First Lady of Uganda. She has been very effective and very visible and has used her role very well in promoting abstinence programmes. Because she is the First Lady, she has a certain celebrity about her that gives her access and visibility.'

The American commitment to abstinence campaigning alarmed some of Uganda's own public health experts. They were not opposed to the campaigns, but they stressed that it was a balanced approach to Aids prevention that had won Uganda its famous success against Aids. Dr David Serwadda, the man who had worked on the earliest signs of the epidemic in the 1980s, told me: 'Donors have tied their activities to certain interventions and that's becoming a major problem. People are getting confused and asking, "What about condoms?" That's because it's the wife of the President and she has got a lot of friends on Capitol Hill who are playing up this controversy. They are directly funding her programme.'

Was there going to be a cost in lives for this confusion? United States aid was keeping HIV-positive people alive through drugs treatment and that was admirable. It was also funding initiatives with the target of preventing 165,000 infections by 2008. Lives might be saved through American-funded prevention initiatives, but could others be lost because of US prescriptions on abstinence-only programmes?

Before I left Kampala, I called on another of Uganda's public health heroes. Dr David Apuuli is perhaps the most impressive of them all. Quietly spoken, he has had to focus through long and exhausting days on the reality, not the politics, of the epidemic. In personal terms he has been profoundly affected. He has lost three brothers and a sister to the disease as well as a number of cousins and other relations, and he has had to bear the responsibility for many Aids orphans.

Dr Apuuli was director of Uganda's national hospital in the late 1980s and witnessed the wards filling up with Aids cases.

He became the country's director of medical services and then the head of the Aids commission in 1999. Like the other Ugandan public health experts I met, Dr Apuuli was convinced that it was a rounded response to the epidemic – abstinence and fidelity, of course, but also condoms 'as a new armament to fight the war' – that had brought the Ugandan prevalence figures down.

And the price of the current conflict? 'I say one thing,' said Dr Apuuli. 'This debate adds only to the suffering and death. If by this debate more people are getting infected and dying, we are doing a disservice to mankind. All those who say that abstinence doesn't work are wrong. All those who say that condoms don't work are wrong. They merely contribute to more deaths. There is a place for each and we should encourage all of them.'

4

A State of Denial

'We got there, but we got there painfully.
We bled every step of the way.'

Dr Nono Simelela, former head of South Africa's Aids programme

The basic facts of the case are as follows. On the evening of 1 April 1999 Charlene Smith, a white South African, was raped at knifepoint at her home in Johannesburg. The rapist was Johannes Thembekile Zinto, a black South African, who was caught and put on trial in December 1999. He was found guilty and sentenced to thirty years in jail, fifteen for the rape and fifteen for theft. Case closed? Not by a long way. The political reverberations from this assault lasted for years and defined a vital aspect of South Africa's immense Aids crisis.

Charlene Smith is a freelance journalist and did what journalists do. She wrote about her experience. In fact she started writing about it the day after the rape on Good Friday, 1999. It took her four days to finish the article and it was published in the *Mail and Guardian* in Johannesburg. It began: 'Every 26 seconds in South Africa a woman gets raped. It was my turn last Thursday night.'

The power of the article, even now, lies not only in the traumatic details of the attack but in the way in which Charlene Smith dissected the official medical response. As with needle-stick injuries for hospital staff, a course of drugs begun immediately after exposure to sexually transmitted HIV significantly reduces the chances of acquiring the virus. Charlene Smith was eventually prescribed a cocktail of three drugs which have the effect of reducing by as much as four-fifths the possibility of infection, but on the night of the rape she was in desperate search for AZT, one of the earliest drugs introduced to counter Aids. The first hospital she was taken to refused her the drug because her medical insurance covered hospitalization only, not out-patient care.

The office of the district surgeon also refused help because it was not government policy to prescribe these drugs to rape victims. 'The rapist bestows a death sentence,' Charlene Smith wrote in her article, 'and the state, by refusing to give cheap medication that could save many women, becomes executioner.'

Charlene Smith did not acquire HIV. The rapist turned out not to be infected.

The *Mail and Guardian* article released an avalanche of concern and publicity for Smith and other victims of rape. She went on to write a book called *Proud of Me* in which she told the stories of other rape victims – and their families – who came to her with moving accounts of their ordeals and how they had remained silent out of fear or shame.

That was not all Charlene Smith did. She describes herself in her book as 'absent-minded, anxious, cranky, eternally broke', but she is also a tenacious reporter who spotted in her own experience a story of sex and violence that constitutes one of South Africa's greatest fault lines in the era of Aids.

The statistics show that South Africa has the worst record

for rape in the world. South Africa also has the world's biggest Aids epidemic, and that adds another terrifying dimension to the scourge of sexual violence.

It would not be long before Thabo Mbeki, the new President of South Africa who succeeded Nelson Mandela in the year that Charlene Smith was raped, would add a further element to the mix, and the most combustible of all – race.

In the original newspaper article, Smith was measured on the matter of race. She wrote about the help she received on the night of the rape from her white and black neighbours. 'I tell you the race of my neighbours because I want you to know that rape is not about race, as some South Africans think. It is not about what men do. It is about what a few sick individuals do, it has nothing to do with race or malehood.'

She later developed a more forthright analysis of what was going wrong in South Africa. In June 2000 she had a piece published in the *Washington Post*, timed to coincide with a visit by Thabo Mbeki to the United States, in which she wrote: 'We won't end this epidemic until we understand the role of tradition and religion – and of a culture in which rape is endemic and has become a prime means of transmitting the disease, to young women as well as children.'

The South African figures show that pre-teen and teenage girls are at disproportionately grave risk of sexual attack, and their young bodies make them physiologically even more vulnerable to acquiring the Aids virus.

Smith attacked Mbeki in person in the *Washington Post* for his failure to endorse the scientific consensus on HIV and Aids, including the merits of antiretroviral drugs, and declared: 'Aids is Thabo Mbeki's Achilles' heel – the man who would lead Africa from the misery of economic poverty will, if his policies continue, preside over graves.' The article ended with a reference to 'chief undertaker Mbeki'.

The immediate consequence of this piece was that President Mbeki was greeted in Washington by demonstrators waving placards bearing the words 'Chief Undertaker Mbeki'. 'He was understandably annoyed,' Ms Smith told me, 'but I'm not apologetic about that at all.'

Mbeki and Smith were once good friends. They knew each other in Lusaka, the Zambian capital, in the final days of South Africa's apartheid regime. He was a nationalist politician in exile; she was a committed journalist writing on resistance politics. They stayed friends after the return of the exiles in the early 1990s. But the friendship between politician and journalist did not long survive the African National Congress coming to power in 1994.

Their differences became personal and bitter in the course of 2000. It was race that lit the fuse. Referring to the wounding article in the *Washington Post* President Mbeki said that 'Charlene Smith was sufficiently brave, or blinded by racist rage, publicly to make the deeply offensive statement that rape is an endemic feature of South African society.' He returned to the charge a few weeks later to accuse her of making 'a nakedly racist statement'.

Charlene Smith has acknowledged that the *Washington Post* sharpened up her piece in subbing it for publication, but she has given no ground whatsoever on the essentials of her difference with Thabo Mbeki. By representing the argument as one about racism, she told me, the President had been 'reasonably successful in deflecting criticism of men and the role of men'.

The problem was a matter of men's sense of entitlement towards women in South Africa, she said. 'If a man sees what he wants, he can take it. That attitude is the father of rape.' She said that Mbeki himself had displayed such an attitude towards women. 'He's a person in a leadership position. We really need African leadership to stand up and say that the way men treat women is unacceptable. And the way children are treated is absolutely unacceptable and has to be changed.'

The dispute between Mbeki and Smith became more bitter as time went on. Mr Mbeki's language certainly became less presidential. In 2004, in response to new crime statistics and a further newspaper article from Smith entitled 'Rape has become a sickening way of life in our land', the President told Parliament that he would not keep quiet 'while others whose minds have been corrupted by the disease of racism, accuse us, the black people of South Africa, Africa and the world, as being, by virtue of our Africanness and skin colour – lazy, liars, foul-smelling, diseased, corrupt, violent, amoral, sexually depraved, animalistic, savage – and rapist'.

Smith raised the temperature another few degrees when she told a university audience in Durban in 2005 that the President was directly complicit in South Africa's high incidence of sexual violence. 'Violence against women has no limits when presidents attack rape survivors and defend men who behave badly,' she said. 'This is not personal, Mr President, this is political.'

The argument between President and journalist had not begun in differences over what was driving South Africa's Aids epidemic, but in how to respond to it. It involved another extraordinary exchange, this one on email between the President and Tony Leon, the leader of South Africa's parliamentary opposition, over whether the drug AZT should be given to rape victims. Leon said that it should be, and Mbeki said that it should not. The correspondence ran to thirty pages.

Thabo Mbeki's contention was that AZT had not been specifically licensed for use in South Africa in cases of rape and that the pharmaceutical company that made it was seeking simply to promote sales. 'I imagine all manufacturers of antiretroviral drugs pay great attention to the very false figures about the incidence of rape in our country,' the President wrote.

At the root of his objections to AZT was the belief that the very drugs that had been keeping HIV-positive people alive in the West were not the answer to South Africa's Aids crisis. Mbeki was not even convinced of the link between HIV and Aids. He appeared to believe that there was a specifically African set of explanations for the continent's Aids crisis which included poverty and malnutrition, and that home-grown solutions were therefore needed.

Thus was born the era of 'Aids denialism' in South Africa, the single gravest act of political negligence in the history of the global epidemic.

It started on the Internet. Surfing the net is one of Mbeki's pastimes. It was there that he convinced himself of the dangers of drugs like AZT and explored the dissident challenges in the West to the long-accepted scientific wisdom that HIV exists, that it is spread in blood and other bodily fluids, that it causes Aids, that it can treated but not cured and that its spread can be prevented, notably through a change in sexual conduct and the use of condoms. The Internet is full of contrary views, if you look for them. In his email correspondence with Tony Leon, Mbeki even advised the leader of the opposition to 'inform himself as extensively as possible about the Aids epidemic ... I would like to recommend that you access the Internet'.

A sign of the new President's serious intention to challenge the conventional science on Aids was his decision in early 2000 to set up an 'International Panel of Scientists on HIV/Aids in Africa'. The panel had a supposedly balanced representation between mainstream and dissident scientists and may genuinely have been aimed at identifying some appropriately 'African' response to the Aids disaster. But the effect was a fateful undermining of national effort and focus. Mbeki was warned of this outcome at the outset.

Professor Malegapuru Makgoba, at that time South Africa's most senior medical research scientist, is one of the public health heroes thrown up by the Aids crisis. They are the ones who have stood up for truth against obfuscation and for bold measures against compromise, consensus and discretion. They have often risked opprobrium and sometimes their livelihoods. Given the enormity of the present Aids catastrophe, it is hardly surprising that there are so few of them.

When I met Professor Makgoba in 2005, he was a university vice-chancellor in Durban, but at the time President Mbeki launched his inquiry into Aids, he was president of South Africa's Medical Research Council. His background gave him the basis for sound judgements on Aids in South Africa. As a doctoral student at Oxford in 1982 he had heard an American epidemiologist describe the early phases of what would be identified as Aids, and had recalled his time as a medical student in South Africa when he saw his first cases of the cancer Kaposi's Sarcoma. He wondered aloud at the Oxford seminar whether this disease was already present in South Africa.

President Mbeki wanted Makgoba's endorsement of his investigation into the science behind Aids. Two thick volumes of dissident literature arrived at the research council, and Makgoba was asked for his response. He was as polite as he could be, but he was emphatic in his dismissal of the dissidents. 'I am fully convinced of the current linkage of HIV infection and the development of Aids,' he wrote to the President in January 2000, and he spelt out the terrible damage that this flirtation with Aids dissidence could do to South Africa. 'It will set back all the efforts we have so far put into this epidemic; it will represent a form of national denial by default; it will be extremely costly for the country in the short and the long term and we shall become the laughing stock, if not the pariah, of the world again.' Those warnings were ignored and those chilling prophecies came close to fulfilment.

Beyond South Africa, Thabo Mbeki made an international pitch to try and persuade others that he was right to reopen the debate on the science of Aids. In a round robin to world leaders including President Clinton, Prime Minister Tony Blair and the United Nations Secretary-General Kofi Annan, which was leaked by the White House, he said that it would be 'absurd and illogical' for Africa to adopt the Western approach to Aids.

Professor Makgoba saw red this time, and at 2 o'clock one morning sat down to write an article for the American journal *Science.* It was entitled 'HIV/Aids: the peril of pseudoscience' and concluded: 'We present South Africans cannot afford to make any more mistakes lest history judges us to have collaborated in one of the greatest crimes of our time.' Makgoba told me that in the piece he submitted he had used the word 'genocide', but his editors at *Science* took it out.

Predictably Mbeki's international commission on Aids managed only to confirm the dissidents in their increasingly discredited views and the conventional scientists in theirs. It did of course cost a lot of money to fly experts from both camps in and out of South Africa – some insisted on flying First Class and treated senior South African health officials as their personal secretaries and travel agents – but it cost the country a lot more in terms of delay and distraction in responding to the mounting Aids death toll.

I was given a telling insight into the commission's workings by Dr Nothemba (Nono) Simelela who from 1999 until her final exasperated resignation in 2004 was head of South Africa's national Aids programme. We met in London at the offices of the International Planned Parenthood Federation in May 2005, and she spoke quietly and sadly about that lost period.

'I sat at these meetings and I listened to these international scientists failing to agree on anything,' said Dr Simelela. 'Somebody would say, "We've identified the virus, we've got pictures of it." Somebody else would say, "No, you never saw the virus, I was in the same lab as you, and you never saw the virus." The dialogue became pathetic. They were swearing at each other on email; they were calling each other names. Some of the emails we had to mediate were scary.

'I thought it was quite tragic that we had people who were discussing this in a country where the evidence was so stark. Why aren't we coming to the present? Why don't we just try and understand why so many people are dying? And these scientists were coming from countries where people were alive because they were getting treatment.'

Dr Simelela's conclusions on the Mbeki Aids initiative were all the harsher for the soft-spoken way in which they were delivered. 'One can't underestimate how much it diverted our attention and slowed us down,' she told me. 'They had wasted money. We still hadn't got an answer and people were still dying.'

The Aids apocalypse reached South Africa late. While the epidemic rampaged around the Western world and took off in so many African countries during the 1980s, in South Africa it was primarily confined to white male homosexuals. The first case among black South Africans was not confirmed until 1987. Professor Makgoba told me: 'Up to that time, whatever else it did, apartheid appeared to isolate South Africa from the rest of the world.'

Among its many crimes, however, apartheid had already warped the nation's response to the disease. It could even help explain Thabo Mbeki's inability to see Aids for what it was – an overwhelming public health problem. In the early 1990s stories circulated that Aids was a conspiracy against blacks. Some seriously believed that it was a sort of final apartheid solution to the advance of black power. That idea led to the adaptation of the Aids acronym to 'Afrikaner Invention to Deprive Us of Sex'.

At the time of Nelson Mandela's release from prison in 1990 South Africa's HIV rate stood at 0.7 per cent. By 1992 it had trebled to 2.2 per cent. By the time South Africans voted in their first free elections in 1994 it had trebled again to 7.6 per cent. When Nelson Mandela stepped down and Thabo Mbeki took over in 1999 it had trebled once more to 22.4 per cent. These shocking figures cannot even hint at the volume of human suffering and grief underlying them. And they kept rising. By 2004 the figure stood at around 26 per cent. With more than 5 million people living with HIV, South Africa is judged to have the largest epidemic in the world.

When the African National Congress assumed power in 1994, everything seemed in place for an effective response to the growing Aids emergency. The ANC's main election document said that its programme to combat sexually transmitted diseases and Aids 'must include the active and early treatment of these diseases at all health facilities' and that there would be mass education programmes. The new government did indeed commit more resources to the Aids fight, but it failed to provide the one thing that experience everywhere has shown is the prerequisite for a proper assault on the epidemic – leadership from the top.

The man who failed to provide that leadership was by popular consent the greatest man on earth.

In interviews after he left power Nelson Mandela was pressed on his response to Aids and, being the man he is, he came clean. In November 2002 at the Dorchester Hotel in London he recorded an interview with David Dimbleby for a two-part BBC television documentary *Mandela – the Living Legend*. He recalled that he had tried raising the issue in the 1994 elections but found his audience 'looking at each other horrified'. He went on: 'At the end of the meeting they walked up to me. "Mr President," meaning President of the ANC at that time, "how can you talk like this? Do you expect us to tell our children to have sex with, what are those things of yours?"

'I say, "Condoms." "Do you expect us to talk about those things?" They were really offended.'

He told how he had visited a high school in Bloemfontein during the campaign and had asked the woman principal whether in his speech he could talk about Aids as well as education. She begged him not to do so because he might lose the election. 'I was not prepared to lose an election and I didn't talk about Aids then,' Mandela told his interviewer.

A month later David Dimbleby interviewed Mandela again for the same documentary portrait and returned to the subject of Aids. Again the former President said how difficult it was to talk about sex in a conservative society, adding this time that there were so many other nation-building priorities crowding in on him during his years in office.

Significantly, though, he endorsed without equivocation Thabo Mbeki's international commission on Aids research and thus the relationship with the dissidents. He did so without reservation, he said, because of the difference between Europe and Africa. 'We are faced with lack of education, with terminal diseases; we must conduct our own researches and find out whether the conclusions in Europe and the United States and Canada are applicable in our case. A government which fails to do so would be foolhardy.'

Nelson Mandela's position could charitably be explained by an anxiety not to second-guess or embarrass his successor. After leaving office he generously lent his name to the cause of Aids awareness. He regularly wore the red ribbon, and his charitable foundations undertook fine work both in Aids education and among Aids orphans. Then in January 2005 he sombrely and courageously announced in public that his son Makgatho had died of the disease. So great is the stigma associated with Aids in South Africa that Makgatho had delayed both an acknowledgement of his condition and the treatment that could have saved his life.

From his years in power, though, South Africans deserved better from Nelson Mandela. Like his friend Bill Clinton, he championed the cause of Aids awareness most openly when he was no longer in a position to dictate the official response. Like Clinton, he dedicated time, energy and his great reputation to raising the profile of Aids and in important humanitarian interventions – but only after his retirement. That was not the role the Aids disaster demanded of world leaders. The record shows that both Mandela and Clinton ducked the issue when they were in a position to do something decisive about it.

In response to rising popular agitation and to serious legal challenges, the South African government began in 2002 to make antiretroviral drugs available for short-term treatment. They announced in April that year that drugs would be provided as prophylaxis in cases of rape and to HIV-positive mothers to prevent them passing the virus to their babies. After more agitation and more legal cases, the government announced in November 2003, five months before President Mbeki was to face the electorate again, a 'comprehensive plan' to make antiretrovirals available throughout the country so that HIV-positive people could be treated to prevent full-blown Aids.

'We got there, but we got there painfully,' Dr Nono Simelela, head of the government's Aids programme throughout that bitter period, told me. 'We bled every step of the way.'

As Thabo Mbeki's second presidential term got under way in April 2004, the official view was that there was a comprehensive Aids plan in place which would now be fully implemented. Many in South Africa who had lived through the years of denial were desperately anxious to believe it. On my visit to research this book in 2005 I was told more than once that the corner had been turned. It probably had. But the foot-dragging, the ambivalence, the half-heartedness had not gone away. For President Mbeki and those closest to him the argument over the cause of Aids had still not been finally settled.

There was a strong indication of this at a World Health Organization conference in Durban in April 2005 concerned with nutrition and HIV/Aids. None of the experts there doubted that a good diet and healthy living contribute to delaying the onset of Aids among HIV-positive people by slowing the breakdown of the immune system. Indeed every single Aids treatment programme that I visited in Africa and elsewhere emphasized the point to its patients. That does not mean that decent nutrition is an alternative to antiretroviral treatment. Yet that is exactly what South African ministers have kept suggesting.

The Durban conference was opened by South Africa's Minister of Health, Dr Manto Tshabalala-Msimang, who had diligently followed her President's line on Aids from the time she was appointed in 1999. Her opening remarks made no reference to the controversies, supposedly left behind, over the causation of Aids in Africa, but at a reception afterwards she was less guarded. She told the crowd that she felt 'vindicated' that the world was finally acknowledging the importance of poverty and malnutrition to Aids, and added exultantly: 'Our President was right all along.'

At the time President Mbeki was visiting Singapore. There he was asked about the Aids controversy in South Africa. He said he hoped there would no longer be controversy, but he added that the WHO Durban conference had underlined the critical importance of nutrition. 'One of the things we have raised was that it is clear and simple – it's in the medical textbooks – it's quite clear that the issue of poverty is one of the issues central to the fight against Aids.' Again, there is no dispute that poverty exacerbates Aids. Its removal, if governments would only get on with it, would diminish the Aids crisis immeasurably. Until then, even then, drugs are the answer for HIV-positive people in Africa just as they have been the answer in the rest of the world.

Mbeki's health minister is now much disliked by the Aids practitioners of South Africa. She is regularly dismissed as 'Dr Garlic' for her commitment to herbal responses to infection. Dr Tshabalala-Msimang did her medical training in Leningrad, in the old Soviet Union, and she has another degree in public health from Antwerp. In her years of exile as an ANC activist she worked as a doctor in half a dozen African countries.

Her enthusiasm for non-conventional medicine extended in 2005 to support for the highly controversial figure of Matthias Rath, a German doctor who runs a California-based foundation promoting vitamins as a treatment for Aids and other diseases.

Dr Rath's commercial activities have come under official scrutiny in a number of European countries and in the United States. In South Africa he launched a grotesque campaign against antiretroviral drugs (claiming they are poisonous and that they kill rather than treat) and the non-government organizations that promote them (claiming they are in the pocket of the drugs companies), a campaign which was condemned by the United Nations agencies as 'wrong and misleading'. In South Africa Dr Rath has received a generous measure of protection from the government.

Dr Tshabalala-Msimang told Parliament that she had had a meeting with Dr Rath in April 2005 in which they discussed 'his concern for the people infected with HIV and suffering from the impact of Aids' and that she would distance herself from him only 'if it could be demonstrated that the vitamin supplements he prescribed are poisonous for people infected with HIV'. The Minister told one newspaper that the Rath foundation was not 'undermining government's position. If anything they are supporting it. Our own programme talks about vitamins and micronutrients.'

I went to see the Minister at her home outside Pretoria, and she answered my questions for well over an hour. Everything she said about the importance of good nutrition (and she said a great deal) seemed to me as a layman to be entirely plausible, although I did wonder how successful she was going to be in delivering better nutrition to South Africa's poor. Dr Tshabalala-Msimang also spoke enthusiastically about what have been described by some as her 'salad dressing' therapies. She mentioned lemon, mint and garlic, with particular emphasis on garlic, which she said had both anti-bacterial and anti-viral properties.

Our exchanges became more tense whenever I pressed her on the question of ARVs, the antiretroviral drugs. She accused me at one point of coming to South Africa to market these drugs, and said she believed that the world's new commitment to providing them for poor people was bound up with a commercial drive to sell them. 'I want to repeat – ARVs do not cure, they just boost the immune system. So if you can get other things that boost your immune system without the side effects that are experienced with ARVs, why not go for those?'

I thought I should establish whether the government had moved on from the 'denialism' that characterized the first Mbeki term. Untreated HIV leads to Aids, doesn't it? 'Not necessarily,' the Minister replied. 'There are people who live for twenty or twenty-five years, and they do not have Aids-defining illness.' Only insignificant numbers, surely? 'But some of them get ill for a time, they manage their illness, and they're fine again. You can't say it leads necessarily to Aids.'

Something else emerged from my meeting with the Minister that might help explain South African resistance to the accepted science of Aids treatment – a strong sense of resentment over the way the government was being advised, or told, by others how to respond to the crisis. Some of those demanding more action were South African, others were foreigners. The Minister singled out the World Health Organization. It had criticized South Africa's failure to do enough towards meeting the global target of 3 million people on treatment by the end of 2005. 'There's an element of arrogance in that,' she said.

She also complained about President Bush's Aids programme which has set itself the target of putting 2 million people on anti-Aids treatment by the end of 2008. Of these 2 million, fully a quarter are expected to come from South Africa. By September 2005, 60,000 were on antiretrovirals in the South African public health sector, only a proportion of them as a result of American help.

This formal US target of 500,000 had created tension between US health officials and their South African counterparts. 'I just take issue with people setting targets for South Africa in our absence,' said the Minister. 'I don't think that's correct ... we are the government of this country, we've got to define policy for this country and we've got to do things in response to the needs of the people of this country.'

President Mbeki's problems with the international Aids consensus went deeper. He seemed to regard the world's alarm over death and suffering from a sexually transmitted disease as a racist commentary on African male sexuality. He even objected to the established view that Aids had its origins in central Africa where the virus is thought to have jumped from primate to man, probably through the preparation of meat. In the email exchanges with the leader of the opposition already quoted, Mbeki referred to these 'wild and insulting claims' and told Leon that he had failed to understand 'the significance of this and the message it communicates to Africans'.

Sex and race appeared to be his twin hang-ups. In a famous speech to a university audience in 2001, the President accused community leaders who demanded more attention be paid to Aids of being convinced that 'we are but natural-born, promiscuous carriers of germs, unique in the world, they proclaim that our continent is doomed to an inevitable mortal end because of our unconquerable devotion to the sin of lust'. Whatever else the President may have achieved with such language, it was surely not national leadership on Aids.

Throughout Mbeki's first term, the bold figure of Malegapuru Makgoba provided scientific counterpoint to the President's agitated rhetoric. He underlined the consequences of South Africa's poor response to Aids by drawing a parallel with Thailand's achievements. In 1990, he said, the HIV prevalence rate in each country stood at 0.7 per cent. A decade later, thanks to strong leadership, the Thai figure had stabilized at less than 2 per cent while in South Africa it had risen to more than 20 per cent. 'We all know that this is a sexually transmitted disease and that's the bottom line,' he told an American Aids conference in 2001, 'and we're doing everything except focusing on the real major factor that determines whether or not you get the disease.'

Professor Makgoba paid a price for his criticism of the government. One letter he received from a senior ANC figure accused him of 'betraying his race', of not being a 'real' black person and of engaging in 'character assassination' of the President. A man who was once Mbeki's favourite scientist was now frozen out. Makgoba told me: 'I was vilified. I was intimidated. I was told to leave the country. I received anonymous telephone calls, and I was called in by ministers to be given a dressing-down.'

I met Malegapuru Makgoba in London on his way home from an Aids conference in Washington. I had two specific questions to put to him. The first was how he accounted for President Mbeki's sensitivity about Aids, and the second was his view of the human cost of South Africa's failure to respond effectively. His answer to the first presented a new twist for those outsiders who have tried to fathom the mind of Thabo Mbeki.

Professor Makgoba began by pointing out that it was only in the 1990s that Aids took off in South Africa, up to a decade later than elsewhere in southern and eastern Africa. This was the decade in which the country was opening up after the isolation of the apartheid years, an era of great mobility within South Africa and across its borders.

Then he posed his own provocative question: 'Did the ANC in addition to bringing liberation also bring Aids? Nobody wants to address this, and this may be at the heart of the policy difficulty. Members of the liberation army lived in these countries where there was high prevalence. It may explain why there is this denial – that the very movement that brought us freedom might also have brought us something that we don't want to talk about.

'The other thing is that you are dealing with people in the army. Everybody knows what armies get up to when they get free. But nobody wants to interrogate that.'

He said that President Mbeki had a blind spot about Aids, and that it was likely to be connected to the ANC's long years in exile. 'If I had been in the liberation struggle fighting for freedom and I come back home and suddenly I bring this in addition to liberation, I would react in this way.'

In the view of Professor Makgoba, South Africa's deeply flawed response to Aids has cost millions of lives. A political biography of Thabo Mbeki by the South African journalist William Mervin Gumede, published in 2005, also concluded that his placing of an entire nation in denial had 'needlessly taken the lives of millions of its citizens'.

Actuarial accuracy will never be achieved, but the lives lost extend well beyond those who could have been saved through drug treatment. President Mbeki's decision to keep questioning the fundamentals of the epidemic undermined education, prevention and condom promotion efforts. If the President himself did not believe in the link between HIV and Aids, why bother to protect yourself from the virus? History will be very harsh on Thabo Mbeki for his handling of the Aids disaster, but the cost to a politician's reputation is nothing compared to the price paid in death and suffering by the people of South Africa.

5

The Lazarus Effect

'I'm an atheist, but I have to say Médecins Sans Frontières was a godsend.'

Zackie Achmat, founder of South Africa's Treatment Action Campaign

Out of Cape Town and past the airport you come to the sprawling township of Khayelitsha, home to around 500,000 people. If you then find the Site B Day Hospital, look for a nondescript sign that says 'To the TB Clinic'. This is in fact one of eight clinics providing HIV/Aids services to the people of Khayelitsha, and discretion is not as necessary as it once was. The waiting-room was full to bursting point on the day I visited, and everyone there was HIV-positive. They seemed to be relaxed and cheerful, and there was animated chatter. Remarkably, everyone looked quite well.

The Site B clinic is run by the charity Médecins Sans Frontières (MSF) which put its first Khayelitsha Aids patient on antiretroviral drugs in 2001. Outside South Africa's private health insurance market, this was the first time that anyone had been treated free with antiretrovirals in the country's public health system. It was one of a number of achievements that have marked MSF out as one of the most impressive international organizations in the Aids field. If MSF had not already won the Nobel Peace Prize for its humanitarian work in 1999, it would surely have deserved it for the significance of its work in South Africa.

Dr Eric Goemaere, the Belgian who runs MSF in South Africa, wanted a single consulting-room at the Day Hospital where he could start seeing patients. The sister in charge told him: 'Doctor, you know in our culture people don't like to be identified as HIV-positive, so they will never queue up in front of your door.' Dr Goemaere replied: 'Sister, I don't know about your culture. In my culture people hate being identified as HIV-positive, but they are desperate to survive as well.' The doctor got his consulting-room, and the queues became so long that after two months they had to construct the special new 'TB' clinic next door.

'That was exclusively for HIV people, so there was very high stigma,' Dr Goemaere told me. 'Of course they hate it, but then you don't want to die. You want to survive. If you create the service, they choose the service despite the stigma.'

The MSF clinic in Khayelitsha practises tough love. HIV-positive people often need to change their behaviour if they are to give themselves a fighting chance of survival, even on the antiretroviral treatment. These drugs are also for life, and there is no giving up on them just because you feel a bit better. Patients must inform at least one person at home of their positive diagnosis so that they can be supported in keeping to the strict treatment regime. Making sure all this happens is the job of a small army of counsellors.

I met Nelisa, one of the 'adherence counsellors' at the Khayelitsha clinic. It was her job to keep patients on the straight and narrow. Like so many of the Aids counsellors I spoke to in South Africa, she displayed exactly that combination of concern, engagement and matter-of-factness that you would hope for in a counsellor. I thought then that if ever I had to be counselled on something as traumatic as an HIV diagnosis, I would like to be counselled by Nelisa.

She told me about the little lectures she gives people on how a healthy lifestyle complements the drugs – no smoking; no drinking; and (a new verb) the need 'to condomize'. 'Husbands and wives, like it or not, I tell them they have to condomize,' said Nelisa. She also said that people on the drugs have to be sure to take them every twelve hours. 'It's no good leaving it for an hour or two. I tell them that HIV is running around their bodies just looking for a gap in their defences.'

When patients start to feel better, there is a period at around six months when they may give up on treatment and stop attending their community support group. Nelisa won't have that. 'I take the clinic car and go and find them. I'll phone first, and if they don't want to be seen with the clinic car, they will come out and find me – and the next day they turn up at the support group!'

All this has worked in Khayelitsha just as it has worked in the other South African clinics where antiretrovirals are finally and slowly – far, far too slowly – being distributed. 'I see people change on ARVs,' said Nelisa. 'It's not just in their personal behaviour. They begin to take responsibility for themselves, they go out and get a job. When they start on ARVs, they don't believe it can help, but then they start gaining weight and feeling much better.'

In the rich world, Aids drugs have been keeping HIV-positive people alive for a decade. In the poor world, where there was once despair, there is now some hope. Often the transformation can be wonderfully rapid. Doctors who witness this have coined the phrase 'the Lazarus effect'.

By September 2005, there were 60,000 people receiving antiretroviral drugs through the South African public health system, but that was only a fraction of those who needed them. South Africa has the largest number of HIV-positive people in the world (more than 5 million) and it is reckoned that up to 1 million of them should be on the drugs. Otherwise they will simply die. South Africa's death toll from Aids is about 250,000 a year.

I have seen busy city Aids clinics in the best hospitals in South Africa gearing up to test, assess and treat the patients who come to them worried that they may be HIV-positive. But in the rural areas and the less favoured townships, the picture is bleaker. This is where the impact of government ambivalence and sluggishness has fallen more heavily. No one has argued that all 250,000 who are dying each year could have been saved, but clear-cut leadership and the earlier distribution of drugs during the Mbeki presidency could have saved many of them. The estimate I kept hearing in South Africa was that the cost of political failure is to be measured in hundreds of thousands of lives. But for the intervention of Médicins Sans Frontières and its allies, that figure would be far higher.

Dr Eric Goemaere arrived in Johannesburg from Europe in 1999 just a few months after Thabo Mbeki became President. He was carrying with him a suitcase and a very simple idea. 'Can we use the tremendous success of antiretrovirals in Europe here in Africa?' The barrier of course was price. A year's course of the drugs cost around $12,000 in the rich world. 'We were convinced that this was an artificial price, and the cost must be made lower.' It was a simple enough idea, but its implications were as revolutionary as any in the history of Third World development.

The MSF plan was to start work in the Johannesburg township of Alexandra. Dr Goemaere visited the clinics there, found support for the idea of Aids treatment and reached agreement in principle to start work. He then drove over to Pretoria, the South African capital, to tell a senior Ministry of Health official what MSF planned to do. 'She started shifting in her chair and looking really uncomfortable,' recalled Dr Goemaere, 'and finally she told me, "You can do it, but not with antiretrovirals, that's not our policy." We thought they were going to be the first country with ARVs,' said Dr Goemaere, 'but they blocked me.'

What saved the day was a telephone call with a South African activist called Zackie Achmat who had just started the Treatment Action Campaign (TAC) in Cape Town to press for government delivery of antiretrovirals. Zackie Achmat invited Dr Goemaere to Cape Town and introduced him to the small Aids support project that TAC had begun in Khayelitsha. An alliance was born that would have a profound impact on treatment in South Africa, and in the larger world would signal progress towards the more distant objective that poor people should not through reason of their poverty alone be excluded from good health.

Even a few years ago, the idea of providing sophisticated (and expensive) therapy to the poor was not on the agenda of the official aid agencies. Their response to the growing Aids emergency was a strategy of prevention. Running an Aids project for the BBC in India at that time, I was in that same prevention-only camp. I was wrong, and I was not alone. Dr Goemaere said that influential development institutions in Britain and elsewhere were 'enormously sceptical' about putting poor people on antiretroviral drugs. He was told that fragile health systems could not cope with such sophistication. 'You're bringing heart transplants to facilities that can hardly deliver aspirins,' the agencies said.

The crudest expression of that view came from Andrew Natsios, head of the American government agency USAID. Soon after his appointment by George W. Bush in 2001, Mr Natsios was asked by a congressional committee about the difficulties in getting drug treatment to HIV-positive people in Africa, and he replied: 'People do not know what watches and clocks are. They do not use Western means for telling the time. They use the sun. These drugs have to be administered during a certain sequence of time during the day and when you say, "Ten o'clock," people will say, "What do you mean by ten o'clock?" They do not use those terms in the villages to describe time.'

What Mr Natsios did not know when he made those observations was that within eighteen months the Bush presidency would commit itself to delivering the largest and most sophisticated drugs programme the poor world had ever seen. Antiretroviral therapy would be overwhelmingly the largest component of the Bush programme. And Mr Natsios would run the agency that implemented it until his resignation at the end of 2005.

It was an American official in South Africa who pointed out to me that in fact Africans have a better record of keeping to drug regimes than patients in the developed world. The availability of treatment also makes an important contribution to prevention because it encourages people to get tested and, if they have the virus, not to pass it on. In the year before MSF arrived to work in Khayelitsha, 450 residents came forward for Aids testing. By 2005 the figure was running at 20,000 a year.

Dr Goemaere's simple idea that the price of anti-Aids drugs was artificially high and should be brought down caused serious headaches for the pharmaceutical companies. In the course of 2000 he wrote to the South African managements of six European and American companies holding important drugs patents and asked them if they had any objection to MSF acquiring generic copies of their drugs and distributing them free to their patients. It was, as Goemaere put it (and he giggled as he told me the story), a 'pseudo-naïve' letter, because of course the drugs companies would have very strenuous objections indeed to such a proposal.

Two companies, GlaxoSmithKline (GSK) and Boehringer Ingelheim, both European, replied offering a meeting. GSK wanted the meeting on 'neutral ground' in a Cape Town hotel, but Paul Stewart, the British head of Boehringer Ingelheim, agreed to travel to MSF's down-at-heel clinic in Khayelitsha. Nothing concrete came of either meeting. The companies emphasized their willingness to make one-off gestures of free drugs and to honour the terms of a United Nations discounting arrangement, but they would not countenance the breaking of their patents. For its part MSF demanded savage price cuts. At one point Dr Goemaere wrote to Boehringer Ingelheim saying that MSF would like to use their drug Nevirapine 'provided that your company immediately reduces its price by 96.6% off US wholesale prices'.

Paul Stewart came face to face with Aids at his meeting with Eric Goemaere. 'There was a child sitting alone, an orphan with Aids, waiting on the bench outside for his consultation,' Dr Goemaere recalled. 'Faced with this emotional reality, Paul stopped talking and asked me if he could personally pay for this boy's treatment. I said, "I'm sorry, but this is not the issue here." Maybe later we can deal with the personal issue, but I want to deal with the broader issue of price.'

Médicins Sans Frontières and the Treatment Action Campaign planned the next step of their campaign to draw dramatic attention to the price question. 'I'm an atheist,' said Zackie Achmat, the man behind TAC, 'but I have to say MSF was a godsend.'

Zackie Achmat's political activism began in the anti-apartheid struggle, continued in the gay rights movement after South Africa became free and then focused on Aids. Zackie was diagnosed as HIV-positive in 1990, and by the end of the decade he was suffering regularly from the many 'opportunistic infections' to which people with compromised immune systems are prey. In particular he had a bad case of candidiasis or thrush, a fungal infection of the throat that makes it difficult to swallow and, if not treated, can prove fatal.

Fortunately the pharmaceutical company Pfizer makes the drug Flucanazole which works wonderfully well for thrush. Unfortunately the month-long course which Zackie needed would cost him 3,000 South African rand, about £270, and he was then earning less than £200 a month. Like so many others in the poor world, he could not afford to get well.

Then MSF produced its own figures. In South Africa, each 200 mg Flucanazole capsule cost between £8 and £10, depending where you bought it. A copy of the drug in India cost £1.30. Further east in Thailand authorized laboratories were manufacturing the drug at 15p per capsule. That was more than sixty times cheaper than the South African price. The answer was obvious: get the pills from Thailand.

With the help of MSF Zackie travelled to Bangkok and brought back enough Flucanazole capsules to treat himself and some of his TAC colleagues who, like him, could not afford the South African price. This was a breach of the Pfizer patent and he was questioned on his return by South African officials, but there was now a publicity bandwagon rolling and no action was taken. 'For us that changed the debate around medicines,' Zackie told me, 'and the public support for breaking the law put all the drug companies on the back foot, not just Pfizer.'

Zackie's travels continued. In early 2001, again in alliance with MSF, he went to Brazil which had established an exceptional record in response to Aids by providing antiretrovirals to its HIV-positive population free of charge. The Brazilians were prepared to challenge and keep challenging the pharmaceutical companies on the price issue. In addition, Brazilian government laboratories were copying and manufacturing their own versions of expensive anti-Aids drugs, and with a further blast of publicity Zackie brought back a supply costing about a third of the South African price.

The high-profile scrap in South Africa over Aids drug prices soon assumed international dimensions. The desperation that poor people feel at being sick and yet unable to afford the cost of getting well had so far brought MSF and TAC together in Cape Town. Beyond South Africa a radical consumer group in the United States had been at work for years in the complex area of global patents, and in India a drugs manufacturer was just itching to make his mark on the world.

Jamie Love, director of the Consumer Project on Technology in Washington, is the cleverest person I met in the research for this book. From the mid-1990s he has restlessly travelled the world developing an encyclopaedic knowledge of the way patents and intellectual property rights obstruct the delivery of health to poor people. The great profits of the drugs companies are a symptom of the problem. The problem itself is an international system that has favoured profits over the welfare of the poor and the failure of governments to change it.

In the middle of 2000 Jamie Love had a meeting in London with Dr Yusuf Hamied who is India's leading manufacturer of generic drugs. The medicines he makes are exact copies of expensive Western pharmaceuticals, and their manufacture is legal in India. Dr Hamied's company Cipla specializes in the 'reverse engineering' required to crack the code of foreign pharmaceuticals. Under Indian law it is the process of manufacture, not the product itself, that can be patented.

Dr Hamied had so far been frustrated in his commitment to provide Aids medicine. Under official prodding in India, he had 'reverse-engineered' the early anti-Aids drug AZT for use at home, but India has had an exceptionally poor record in making treatment available for its own millions with HIV, and Cipla's Aids drugs were left on the shelf.

For the international market Cipla manufactured a drug called Triomune which was a copy of three foreign-patented pharmaceuticals combined together in one pill. Instead of eight tablets to be taken each day, Aids patients needed just two Triomunes – one pill at sunrise, one at sunset; ideal for African conditions. Africa wanted Triomune, and Dr Hamied was very keen to get it there in quantity.

When Jamie Love met Dr Hamied in the middle of 2000, Cipla was prepared to sell Triomune for between $600 and $800 per patient per year. It was a huge saving on the $12,000 that the cocktail of three individual drugs would otherwise have cost. But the offer still lacked a truly headline-grabbing quality. That emerged at the beginning of 2001, the result of a very direct question put by Jamie Love to Yusuf Hamied.

'Is there any chance of providing that Aids cocktail at a dollar a day?'

Dr Hamied said there was, and he sent a fax to Médicins Sans Frontières offering them Triomune at $350 per patient per year.

He then got a call from the *New York Times*. 'Is it true that you have offered the Aids cocktail at $350 a year?' Hamied said it was. The reporter, Donald G. McNeil Jr., ended the interview with the words: 'Dr Hamied, from tomorrow your life won't be the same.'

The story appeared on the front page of the *New York Times* on 7 February 2001. 'I'm not joking,' Dr Hamied told me four years later. 'My life has not been the same.'

It was an eye-catching story and a massive breakthrough. The Cipla offer seemed to signal that the days when poverty alone could price poor people out of their health might be numbered. In South Africa in 2001 it set the stage for a court drama which represented the single greatest reverse ever suffered by the pharmaceutical industry.

One of the tasks facing a free South Africa was reform of its health system. Apartheid had led to many grotesque distortions, among them the arrangements that provided First World health care at First World prices for the rich and the white, and very little for poor black South Africans. The purpose of the Medicines Amendment Act of 1997 was to change that – not as radically as some would have liked, but at least to start making drugs affordable for the majority of South Africans. Early in 1998 South Africa's Pharmaceutical Manufacturers Association, representing the international industry, along with up to forty individual companies hit back by suing the South African government over the threat this measure posed to international patents and the world trading order.

As the *Wall Street Journal* pointedly asked at the time: 'Can the pharmaceutical industry inflict more damage on its ailing public image? Well, how about suing Nelson Mandela?'

Shamefully, both the United States government and the European Union backed the pharmaceutical companies in this action. The US used every available diplomatic weapon to force a rethink in Pretoria, including trade sanctions, but South Africa stood firm. Some of its defensive firepower was provided by Jamie Love of the Consumer Project on Technology, who had advised the South African government on the merits of its action from the beginning.

In America the case reached a noisy climax in 1999 as Vice-President Al Gore declared his candidacy for the 2000 presidential election. 'Gore Greed Kills', 'Gore Kills Aids Patients' were not the banners he wanted to see – or wanted the TV crews to film – as he launched his bid for the White House. But it was Gore who had led the diplomatic offensive against South Africa over the Medicines Act, and whatever his own political sympathies Jamie Love was dry-eyed about causing embarrassment to the Democrat candidate: 'Gore wanted to keep things back in the apartheid regime as far as this issue was concerned.'

In due course the US and the EU reversed their position on the South African Medicines Act, with President Clinton declaring that Washington would no longer obstruct African efforts to gain access to affordable HIV drugs. This left the pharmaceutical companies to press on alone with the court case, but they were still confronted by that radical alliance of the Washington Consumer Project, the Treatment Action Campaign and Médicins Sans Frontières.

Over the protests of lawyers representing the pharmaceutical companies, TAC was admitted as a participant in the case in March 2001. The legal process had dragged on now for three years, but within a month of TAC's admission the pharmaceutical companies threw in the towel. It was a famous victory for the government and TAC, and it was a famous defeat for the industry. Its larger significance lay in how Aids was now driving the argument for poor people's access to essential medicines. That broader objective had first motivated South African ministers to frame the Medicines Amendment Act, but South Africa was now living in the era of President Mbeki, his health minister Dr Tshabalala-Msimang and the government's discomfort and denial over Aids.

Eric Goemaere of MSF told me that somewhere he has a photograph of everyone drinking champagne with the Minister to celebrate the court victory. She invited them all to her home for the party. But that was the last time that Aids activists would drink champagne with the Minister. There would be other important court cases in future, but none would be in alliance with the government. Some indeed would be fierce challenges to government resistance over making Aids treatment available.

First of all the Treatment Action Campaign, backed by some brilliant minds at the Aids Law Project in Johannesburg, took on the government over its refusal to give the drug Nevirapine to pregnant women to stop the transmission of HIV to their babies. They pursued the case through the high court to the constitutional court and gained a judgment forcing the government to make treatment available. This was the new South Africa in action – the provisions of a liberal constitution that guaranteed health care upheld by the courts in the face of ministerial objections.

The drugs companies were next in line. In 2002 the Treatment Action Campaign took GlaxoSmithKline and Boehringer Ingelheim to the country's Competition Commission over the 'excessive pricing' of their anti-Aids drugs. These prices were, in the words of the complaint, 'directly responsible for premature, predictable and avoidable deaths of people living with HIV/Aids, including both children and adults'. The commission found that the companies had abused their monopoly and wrongly excluded competitors from the marketplace.

The next step would be a reference to the Competition Tribunal, which had the power to impose a settlement on the companies, but the activists wanted to make the drugs available promptly. Negotiations led to voluntary licences being granted to a number of generic drugs manufacturers to enable them to make copies of the patented medicines. It was another small step towards gaining poor people's access to drugs.

The main complainant in the unfair competition case was a young woman called Hazel Tau. She was HIV-positive, she was getting sicker by the day and she was in desperate need of antiretroviral treatment. On the day the hearings opened, she took part in a press conference and collapsed while making her case. She was taken off to hospital. Her CD4 count, the blood test that establishes the state of a patient's immune system, was down to 9. That compares with a healthy person's count of 500 to 1,500, and the danger level of 200 where antiretroviral treatment becomes essential. Hazel was so emaciated that the doctor had difficulty getting blood from a vein.

I met Hazel Tau in Johannesburg in 2005. Here was the 'Lazarus effect' in action. As a result of that well-publicized collapse at the press conference, an anonymous donor had come forward to sponsor her treatment. The gravity of her condition also led her to overcome her anxiety about the possibly toxic side effects of the drugs, an anxiety created by South Africa's ruinous antiretrovirals-versus-nutrition debate.

Three years on Hazel looked wonderful – a beautiful woman, alluringly dressed, and in full-time work with a sexual health research project at Baragwanath Hospital in Soweto. 'I am proud of myself,' she told me as she recalled her role in the competition case. 'I was very sick at that time, and I didn't realize that ARVs could change people's lives. I thought I was going to die anyway, and so what was it for? But then I thought that even if the case doesn't help me, it can help other people.'

As Hazel regained her health on the antiretrovirals, the man who ran the Treatment Action Campaign was becoming seriously ill. Zackie Achmat had no doubt about the benefit of the drugs, and he knew that his rich friends would pay for them, but he had taken a decision from the time of TAC's foundation that he would not start his own treatment until the government made antiretrovirals available universally. This was Zackie's 'drugs fast', another powerful weapon in the TAC armoury.

Zackie refused drugs for more than four years. In the middle of that period, in 2002, he received a telephone call from Nelson Mandela himself. 'I'm coming to see you and I want you to start taking the medicines,' the former President told him. In awe and admiration of the great man, the activist would like to have obliged, but he told Mandela that he would not end the fast until the government showed a proper commitment to distributing ARVs. It took days to negotiate the terms of the Mandela-Achmat meeting, but it did take place and it had powerful symbolic significance. Nelson Mandela complimented Zackie's principled stand but issued no public appeal for the fast to end, and so received no formal rebuff.

In 2003 the Treatment Action Campaign launched a civil disobedience movement demanding that the government begin full-scale distribution of antiretroviral drugs. The protests were underpinned by further challenges in the courts. Ever since the judgment over mother-to-child transmission, there had been an official commitment on paper to make antiretrovirals available, but in reality there was just more foot-dragging. The civil disobedience campaign led to further unwelcome publicity for the Mbeki government, and Zackie Achmat grew more and more sick.

By the middle of 2003 he was suffering from a lengthening list of illnesses: recurrent respiratory infections, shingles, herpes, thrush. 'My health really started to decline, and everyone was seriously worried that I was going to get TB,' Zackie told me.

At a Treatment Action Campaign conference in August 2003 he was instructed to end his fast. That would not necessarily have changed his resolve if the government had not also shown signs of being worn down by the activists. 'I came round to the position that it would be foolish to kill myself just because of the stupidity and denial of the government,' Zackie said. 'Killing myself was going to be to nobody's advantage but the government's.'

He ended his fast in September 2003, and in November the government unveiled its programme for making antiretroviral therapy available throughout the country. In the months and years that followed, that undertaking was to prove a cruel let-down, and TAC continued with its legal challenges and street protests. A generation of anti-apartheid campaigners was well used to that. What surprised them was their target. 'We never imagined that we would fight with our own government,' Zackie Achmat told me. 'We thought the bigger and longer battle would be with the international pharmaceutical companies. I still believe that will prove to be the case.'

6

Big Pharma, Little Pharma

'This is not a debate between health and trade. We are talking about human rights. It's an ethical debate.'

Dr Germán Velásquez, World Health Organization

President George Bush's State of the Union speech in January 2003 was the one in which he prepared America and the world for the war in Iraq. It was also the one in which he announced his $15 billion commitment to Aids, 'a work of mercy beyond all current international efforts to help the people of Africa'.

Across that continent, he said, 4 million required immediate drug treatment, and only 50,000 were getting it. The American plan would put 2 million of them on antiretroviral drugs in five years – 'seldom has history offered a greater opportunity to do so much for so many'. And why was this tremendous possibility within our grasp? 'The cost of those drugs has dropped from $12,000 a year to under $300 a year.'

In making such a compelling comparison – anti-Aids drugs costing forty times less than they did just a few years before – the President appeared to recognize the validity of 'copy-cat' drugs production around the world and to endorse the activist drive which wanted to make them available throughout Africa. For Big Pharma, it appeared to give the game away.

By the time the Bush Aids programme entered its second full year, it was clear that the President's expectation of big savings on drugs was not being realized. In January 2005, the United States Government Accountability Office produced an emphatic report on the economics of American antiretroviral distribution in Africa.

Because the purchase of antiretrovirals had so far been limited to American-manufactured and patented drugs, it was costing up to $368 *more* per Aids patient per year to deliver help from the United States than it was from anywhere else. Moreover, other international donors had more flexibility in choosing from a range of generic drugs and in supplying the combination pills that were much easier for people to take.

Unless something was done, the Government Accountability Office calculated that over the full five years of the Bush programme American taxpayers could be paying an extra $170 million for every 100,000 people treated in Africa. It meant that fewer patients could be kept alive for the money available and that accordingly more would die.

Despite the President's observations on price in his State of the Union address, the emergency Aids programme appeared from the outset to favour the big pharmaceutical companies and their expensive branded drugs. The programme strategy document in fact complimented Big Pharma for 'responding to the evolution of a market in the developing world' and laid down that drug procurement would have to 'fit within the parameters of existing federal and international law for the protection of intellectual property rights'.

It was only after months of pressure that the policy was amended to allow for the President's Aids programme to buy its drugs from any manufacturer in the world. But they would still have to be approved by America's own regulatory authorities and for this a 'fast-track' process was offered. Only by the end of 2005, almost three years after that State of the Union address, were the first of those cheaper, foreign-made generic anti-Aids drugs beginning to reach patients in Africa under the Bush programme.

Visit any American pharmacy and you will find the shelves full of copy-cat drugs. The generics sit alongside the branded drugs. They are bio-equivalents doing the same job and they cost a lot less. The patent-holder gets fourteen years of exclusive marketing rights, but the day the patent expires, the competition can step in. Half the drugs sold in America are copies, but they represent only 12 per cent of the total dollar value. It is a system that works well enough for America and other rich parts of the world – the patent-holder makes a lot of money during the years of exclusivity, and the price comes down for everyone, eventually.

But the global Aids crisis has raised an immense and public challenge to this system. Poor people in poor countries cannot afford the expensive branded drugs. Without international help, they can barely even manage the cost of generics. Nor can they afford to wait until patents eventually expire. By that time they will be dead.

The international trading system that enabled the big pharmaceutical companies to enforce patents around the world was negotiated in the early 1990s, and it was the gathering Aids crisis that led to those arrangements being questioned. The issue was TRIPS – Trade-Related Aspects of Intellectual Property Rights. At a ministerial meeting of the World Trade Organization in Doha in November 2001 it was agreed that 'the TRIPS Agreement does not and should not prevent members from taking measures to protect public health'.

The Doha Declaration ran to just seven crisp paragraphs and became a key text in the battle to get affordable drugs to poor people: 'Each member has the right to grant compulsory licences and the freedom to determine the grounds on which such licences are granted. Each member has the right to determine what constitutes a national emergency ... it being understood that public health crises, including those related to HIV/Aids, tuberculosis, malaria and other epidemics, can represent a national emergency ...'

The Doha meeting came within weeks of 9/11. After those attacks, there had then been a bioterrorism scare when American postal and media workers had handled anthrax-impregnated mail and died. The US considered issuing a compulsory licence to override a foreign-held patent on a drug for the treatment of anthrax and negotiated major price reductions. America could hardly be prepared to break a drugs patent for its own emergency and then deny poor countries the same right when faced with the continuing emergency of Aids.

But the Doha Declaration was not legally binding, and it did not prevent the United States from seeking other ways to shore up the interests of its pharmaceutical industry. In a series of bilateral trade deals, notably in Central America, the US has managed to secure binding undertakings on the security of pharmaceutical patents in exchange for granting favourable trading status with the world's most powerful economy.

This US strategy came in for extremely sharp criticism at a 2004 international Aids conference in Thailand. Jacques Chirac, the President of France, sent a message to the conference which emphasized the need to step up treatment for the millions who required antiretrovirals, and added: 'Let's implement the generic drug agreement to consolidate price reductions. Making certain countries drop these measures in favour of bilateral trade negotiations would be immoral blackmail.' It is not every day that the United States government is accused of 'immoral blackmail', even by the President of France.

Big Pharma's own objective was to prevent countries from issuing compulsory licences for Aids drugs. Rather like possession of a nuclear bomb, once one country succeeds in issuing a compulsory licence everyone else will want to issue one too. The activists and the campaigners, on the other hand, wanted to prod third countries into issuing these licences because they wanted to start restructuring the drugs industry to benefit the poor. For developing countries themselves, the objective was simply to acquire the drugs at a price that would not break the bank.

It was in South Africa, where so much of this argument had played out, that the pharmaceutical giants came up with a solution that enabled them to comply with local regulations and to retain an essential measure of control at the same time. Big Pharma had so far been up against Generic Pharma, but now there was a new player on the field – Little Pharma.

Aspen Pharmacare had been going for less than a decade when it became the first drug manufacturer in the world to receive US approval to produce antiretrovirals. The company started up in a private house in Durban in 1997 and grew through a series of stunning take-overs to become the largest home-grown drugmaker in Africa. With Big Pharma still at the receiving end of fierce activist pressure and fresh court challenges, GlaxoSmithKline and Boehringer Ingelheim chose to issue voluntary licences for antiretroviral drugs to Aspen.

This sweetheart deal suited everyone very well. Aspen could see the commercial opportunity presented by South Africa's Aids disaster and the even larger catastrophe unfolding beyond its borders. For the multinational companies, the deal involved modest royalty payments, but it also meant that their loss of direct business might be limited to Africa and to the field of Aids. For both sides, it served the larger purpose of insuring that aggressive generic manufacturers like the Indian company Cipla could be excluded from gaining further footholds on the continent.

As a result of these voluntary licences and a 'fast-track' approval process, the US was now in a position to buy Aspen drugs for distribution on the Bush Aids programme throughout Africa. But there was then a hitch that led to further delay and frustration. The national drug regulators of at least four African countries said they would not accept the approval of the United States Food and Drug Administration for the Aspen drugs. Aspen antiretrovirals could not be distributed until local regulations had been satisfied. In these countries, drugs approval was based on the processes of the World Health Organization, and on this there had been a tense and wasteful stand-off for a year or more between the UN body and the US government.

The Bush Aids programme was 'can-do' America in action. It was also 'go-it-alone' America. Whatever the rhetoric from Washington, the reality was that the United States knew best and was unenthusiastic about its own efforts being subsumed by a multilateral approach to global Aids. President Bush's decision to commit $15 billion to fight the disease had the effect of concentrating funds on exclusive US efforts rather than bolstering the programmes of the international agencies. When it came to drugs approval, the US favoured its own regulators and appeared to have no interest in bolstering the international system.

The essential drugs office of the World Health Organization began developing its approval system for Third World medicine in 2001. The poor were as entitled to quality assurance as the rich, and they needed the same level of protection against substandard production and counterfeiting. As in so many other areas, it was the urgency and the enormity of the Aids crisis that propelled WHO to establish a 'pre-qualification' procedure for generic drugs for HIV-positive people.

The man in charge at WHO was Dr Lembit Rägo, a former professor of clinical pharmacology who had rebuilt his native Estonia's drug regulatory system after the end of the Soviet Union. In fashioning the WHO pre-qualification system, he secured the technical backing of some of the leading European regulators. The United States was approached but refused point-blank to lend any expertise from its own regulator, the Food and Drug Administration. The suspicion was that the FDA was more interested in defending the interests of the US pharmaceutical industry than in supporting credible international efforts to make drugs safer in developing countries.

Jamie Love of the Consumer Project on Technology in Washington said this of the FDA decision: 'To me it's unbelievable that health regulators in the US and Europe – particularly in the US – will somehow actively conspire against solving quality regulations for drugs to treat poor people in the poorest countries on earth. To me that's right up there with war-crimes stuff.'

There was already tension between the US and WHO on essential medicines for the poor. Despite WHO's abdication from the fight against Aids in the 1990s – it effectively ceded responsibility to the new programme UNAIDS, and valuable time was lost

– the backroom boys in WHO's essential drugs office in Geneva had been challenging the interests of Big Pharma for years. I encountered more quiet passion and radicalism in those offices than in any other part of the UN system I visited.

Dr Germán Velásquez is a Colombian economist with an over-riding, some might say unreasonable, commitment to providing affordable drugs to the poor. Ever since the original world trade deal of the early 1990s he has used his position in the essential drugs secretariat to press for real action. It has got him into a number of scrapes with Big Pharma and its government allies.

There was, for example, the case of the glossy red book *Globalization and Access to Drugs* which Dr Velásquez co-authored in 1997 as a WHO guide to how poor countries should approach the World Trade Organization rules on intellectual property rights. US representatives were outraged by this crib and got the book withdrawn. It was then farmed out for review by a panel of experts and two years later was reissued by WHO in a 'revised' form virtually identical to the original – except it now had a glossy blue instead of a glossy red cover.

Aids also provided the impetus for the formation of alliances between Dr Velásquez at WHO and more radical organizations outside. When intellectual property rules were reviewed by the World Trade Organization in Doha in 2001 there was elaborate co-ordination with the agency Médicins Sans Frontières whose remarkable work in South Africa had done so much to promote access to treatment for poor people in the first place. 'This is not a debate between health and trade,' Dr Velásquez told me. 'We are talking about human rights. It's an ethical debate. If there are trade rules that are not serving the access to health of all the population, we may be forced to see how to rectify the rules.'

In the run-up to Doha in November 2001 and in the immediate aftermath of the humiliating collapse of Big Pharma's case against the South African government in April that year, Dr Velásquez appeared to pay a heavy price for his activism. On 26 May that year he was assaulted and robbed on his way to a WHO meeting in Rio de Janeiro. He still has the knife scar on his wrist. He put the attack down to Rio's high crime rate until two days later in Miami he was assaulted again by two men who not only referred to the Rio assault but also, according to Dr Velásquez's account to police, warned him off in these terms: 'We hope you learn the lessons of Rio. Stop messing with the pharmaceutical industry.'

This was not the end of it. At his home, just over the Swiss-French border and close to his office in Geneva, he received a number of anonymous telephone calls in which he was specifically told not to attend a forthcoming meeting of the World Trade Organization on intellectual property rights. When he asked who was speaking, the caller referred to Lincoln Road, the street where he was attacked in Miami.

French police built up a large file on the Velásquez case, but there were no arrests. Pharmaceutical industry spokesmen dismissed any idea that it could have been to their advantage to threaten a middle-ranking WHO official, and Dr Velásquez has stopped thinking about the attacks except to offer this speculation: 'After the South Africa case collapsed, I would be surprised if there was not some industry involvement, but of course they would take care to sub-contract, and then sub-contract ...'

Before the Aids disaster, there was very little public attention paid to the idea that poor people should have access to the drugs they needed for survival. The glib assumption was that the era of personal medicine was a long way off for the poorest people and the poorest communities on earth.

Aids changed that public perspective, and the politicians had to respond. But it will not be enough for the US to undertake to put 2 million on antiretrovirals by 2008 and for the G8 leaders to aim to treat everyone in need by 2010. Decrepit health systems in the poor world will have to be rebuilt if such promises are to be honoured. Since anti-Aids drugs must be taken for life, donors have also assumed a moral commitment to keep treating HIV-positive people indefinitely. Furthermore there can be no justification for keeping individuals alive for one well-publicized condition and then refusing them treatment for other equally fatal diseases.

In the early years of the African Aids crisis, Big Pharma appeared to offer few solutions. The pharmaceutical companies were obstacles both to realistic pricing and to proper access to drugs for the poor. But the great clashes between Big Pharma and the activists in South Africa began to prompt fresh thinking. The negative publicity the companies received meant that their corporate reputations were now at stake and they badly needed to restore a tarnished image.

In one key area, for example, differential pricing has taken root so that antiretroviral drugs are offered at far lower prices to poor countries than in the rich world. But there is a big challenge looming. These initiatives have so far centred on the first line of drug defence against Aids. In the rich world, HIV-positive people are already on the second and third lines of defence as the virus mutates and resistance develops. These more sophisticated drugs are up to twenty times more expensive than the original ones. How will patients, governments, donor agencies afford them?

Industry supporters argue that more pressure on Big Pharma to provide more answers to the Aids crisis would be self-defeating. Randall Tobias, appointed by George Bush to head the US Aids programme, was previously CEO of the pharmaceutical giant Eli Lilly and presents this boardroom perspective: 'If you're the CEO of a pharmaceutical company and you have $15–20 billion to invest in research and development, and you have researchers come to you with recommendations to fund programmes for $50 billion, you've got to make choices as to which you'll fund and which you won't. It's just a lot easier in the political environment now surrounding Aids to put your money into breast cancer, cardiovascular disease or diabetes.

'I worry that long after I've gone from this job, I'm going to be reading the *Financial Times* one morning and see a story about how there's only company left in the antiretroviral drug business. We need to insure that there are the financial incentives to keep all this going.'

With Aids representing a global as well as a Third World crisis, few frankly believe that Big Pharma will withdraw from this field. But the response to Aids and other diseases killing people in the poor world is too important and too urgent to be left to the marketplace. At the Aids Law Project in Johannesburg, which mounted those mighty legal challenges to Big Pharma in South Africa, the view is that a purely commercial system will never provide the answer. 'You can tinker, you can challenge it, you can squeeze a little bit out of it,' said Mark Heywood, who heads the project, 'but it's not a system that is geared to researching or producing medicines for developing country diseases because there is no market for those diseases.'

Five years on from the end of the first big legal clash over Aids drugs in South Africa, there is some hope that diseases affecting the poor may be tackled more effectively in future. Alliances are being forged between pharmaceutical companies, major philanthropic institutions like the Bill and Melinda Gates Foundation and rich governments to conduct research into those Third World diseases for which there is no commercial market. This has led to projects involving the major killers malaria and tuberculosis, which are as devastating in their impact as Aids itself, but also less common tropical diseases such as sleeping sickness and elephantiasis. In fact there has already been far more research undertaken on these neglected diseases in the new century than was conducted in the last twenty-five years of the twentieth century.

Having merely defended its commercial position in the early years of the Aids crisis, Big Pharma now has the chance to be part of the solution. These companies have been aggressively backed by the United States and other Western governments in securing favourable patent arrangements and have effectively seen off the commercial threat posed by generic drugs manufacturers from countries like India. But these arrangements now need to work for poor people in poor countries as well as shareholders in the rich world. Affordable versions of second- and third-line antiretroviral drugs have to be delivered, and there have to be results in tackling neglected tropical diseases. Then the battles fought in South Africa at the start of the new century will have been worth fighting.

7

Clerical Errors

'I believe in all the fundamental beliefs of the Church, but I cannot use them to fight a disease.'

Father Valeriano Paitoni, São Paulo, Brazil

On first meeting him, you get little idea of just how big a problem Father Valeriano has been for the hierarchy of the Roman Catholic Church. Bearded, bespectacled and undemonstrative, he does not strike you as a turbulent radical. It is only as his story unfolds that it becomes clear how far this Italian priest has gone in challenging the Vatican view that condoms must not be used to prevent the spread of HIV.

I visited Father Valeriano Paitoni at his handsome parish church in São Paulo, Brazil, and he led me through to a cluttered little office at the back. He began to tell me about a life's journey that had taken him from Brescia in Italy to a Catholic seminary in London and in the 1970s to Brazil as a missionary. When the Aids epidemic struck his first parish, he opened a home for destitutes, people rejected by their families because they were infected and dying. In his present parish, he opened two homes for children who have either been orphaned, abandoned or infected (often all three) through Aids.

At this point in his story, Father Valeriano was called out to attend to a parishioner. I looked around at the pictures of the Holy Family, the little plaster saints, the piles of uplifting tracts. It was as a priest's office should be. Then I noticed a glass frame hung near the door. On it was written in Portuguese 'In case of Emergency, Break the Glass'. Inside was a condom.

One of the children's homes occupies the bottom floors of Father Valeriano's own house. It had once been a residence for four parish priests, but now there is only Father Valeriano, so there is a lot of spare room. The older children were out at school when he showed me round. He beamed at the younger ones and translated a question about whether, since I was British, I was a personal friend of David Beckham.

Only the surgery was a reminder of the children's HIV-positive status. Here the familiar antiretrovirals were laid out for dispensing. This was also where some of the older children came to pick up their condoms. 'So they may be sexually active?' I asked Father Valeriano delicately. 'They *are* sexually active,' he replied with emphasis.

Father Valeriano called the home 'Siloam' after the pool in Jerusalem to which Christ sent the blind man and where his sight was restored. The disciples then asked Jesus whether it was the man himself or his parents who had sinned and caused his blindness. He answered: 'Neither this man nor his parents sinned, but he was born blind so that the acts of God may be revealed through what happens to him.' A fine, non-judgemental text for the era of Aids.

'Siloam' and Father Valeriano's other homes are the caring face of the Roman Catholic Church that shines so brightly in the darkness of Aids. The São Paulo homes are supported entirely from within the parish. They receive no government help, and do not seek it. Nor do they ask for money from the battalions of foreign aid-givers. This is true Christian charity at work. But the relentlessness of the Aids tragedy and its preventability prompted Father Valeriano and a few of his colleagues to take a bolder step to remind the Church of its charitable duty.

In 2000, with the permission of Brazil's Catholic bishops, they arranged a conference of church organizations working with HIV-positive people. The idea was to share experiences and chart a way forward. The Vatican sent Bishop Lozano Barragán to tell the conference about the international dimensions of the Aids crisis. Bishop Barragán is a Mexican and had recently been appointed to head the Vatican department responsible for health-care workers. Father Valeriano thought the Bishop's presence at the conference would be helpful. In the event, he said, it led to 'very deep discussions between us and the authorities in Rome'. In plain language, there was an almighty row.

Father Valeriano had prepared a folder for the conference dealing with Aids prevention. It also had the approval of Brazil's bishops and stressed the need for people to follow what were called 'the evangelical values' of chastity and fidelity. But those who did 'not know how to live up to evangelical values' should use condoms. When Bishop Barragán saw this folder, he banned its distribution, and the organization of Brazilian bishops denied that they had even seen it, far less approved of it.

In his quiet and determined fashion, Father Valeriano remains utterly unapologetic about the trouble he has caused. 'There is a simple starting position,' he told me. 'We have to defend life at any cost. Christ came so that everybody should have life. So in the context of the HIV epidemic the use of the condom is necessary and justified. It should not be condemned.

'I believe in all the fundamental beliefs of the Church, but I cannot use them to fight a disease.

'The great error that the Catholic Church makes is that it does not want to accept the fragility of human beings. That's the opposite of what Christ did – He totally accepted human fragility.

'If Christ was here today, He would be the first to say, "Use the condom." I have no doubt about that.'

The differences between Rome and the modest parish priest in São Paulo were just beginning. Father Valeriano gave an interview to one of the city's big newspapers in which he described parallel churches in Brazil divided between the progressives, working directly with the people, and the conservative hierarchy. As an echo of the struggle over 'liberation theology' in the pre-Aids era in Latin America, this was particularly unwelcome. So was his naming of Dom Claudio Hummes, Archbishop of São Paulo, as one of the key conservatives.

Archbishop Hummes went on local radio to condemn the priest's views on condoms, and from behind the scenes started pressing for his removal. The head of Father Valeriano's order in São Paulo was urged to eject him from the parish, from the city, preferably from the country. 'I told my superior that I would go,' the Father told me, 'provided the Archbishop came in person to my parish and explained to my parishioners why I was going.' He heard no more of plans for his removal.

The Archbishop was concerned about Aids, but he appeared more concerned about the teachings of the Church. He even took on the Aids experts of São Paulo who had led the city's and the country's remarkable fight to contain the disease. Dr Artur Kalichman, now in charge of São Paulo's main Aids treatment centre, recalled attending a public meeting with the Archbishop who declared that condoms had holes in them. By his own account,

Dr Kalichman got to his feet and said: 'Hey, don't do that! I respect your beliefs and I will not ask you to give up your religion. But please don't come up with scientific arguments. I can prove to you there are no holes. Your position is not based on science. It is based on dogma and belief.'

Back in Europe I was keen to go to Rome and interview the bishop who had visited Brazil on the Vatican's behalf. In 2003 he became Cardinal Lozano Barragán, but he retained the portfolio for health-care workers and is one of two cardinals with direct responsibility for Aids. My request was turned down, but his office did send me a letter he had written on the subject of condoms and Aids.

'My thesis is abstinence outside marriage and marriage fidelity,' the Cardinal wrote. 'One should never use preservatives as [a] safeguard from infection in order to have an inordinate exercise of human sexuality.'

So far so dogmatic. Cardinal Barragán allowed one specific exception. A condom could be used 'when the life of an innocent person is in danger due to the aggression of another person,' he said. 'Such may be the case when somebody infected with HIV/Aids forces the partner to have sexual intercourse.'

Some have seen in this a response to the immense and growing problem of 'discordancy' within marriages where one partner has the HIV virus and the other does not. Cardinal Barragán was further quoted around the time of Pope John Paul II's death in 2005 as promoting this more elastic view of condom use within marriage. But in the letter sent to me two months after the accession of Pope Benedict XVI, the Cardinal made no such allowance. To say that a woman may insist on the use of a condom only in the event of sexual assault is, on the face it, absurd as well as offensive.

In São Paulo, Father Valeriano had lost patience with the Vatican. He told me that if Rome had not intervened in the efforts of Brazilian Catholics to respond to Aids, the Church would have reformed its attitude towards condoms long ago. I asked him about lives lost as a consequence. 'I agree that the Roman Catholic Church is fundamentally guilty in all this. It seems that the official position of Rome doesn't accept the human reality – and that is what the Gospel offers us all.'

Accusations of the Church's guilt over Aids found expression in Father Valeriano's next venture – a film for the Millennium. It was called *Defending Life for Another 500 Years* and was made at a time when Brazil was also marking the 500th anniversary of the Portuguese arrival. The parallels he drew would have been provocative if made by a secular film-maker. For a Roman Catholic priest to draw them was incendiary.

The film starts with an account of the Church's apology for its role in the destruction of Indian life and culture in Brazil and for its exploitation of African slaves shipped across the Atlantic. It says that Brazilians with Aids are now discriminated against in the same way that Indians and Africans were once treated. Then it produces the figures for the number of HIV infections prevented (38,000, according to a 1999 estimate) and the link with a 500 per cent increase in condom distribution in previous years.

At this point in the film, a priest's hands present the Host to camera, except that they are not holding consecrated bread but a wrapped condom. No one could complain that Father Valeriano's film lacks directness. It then quotes St John's Gospel: 'I have come so that they may have life, and may have it abundantly,' and adds that condom promotion is the best way to promote life in the era of Aids. 'Help us in the new millennium to defend life in its fullness,' the film concludes, and then it makes a final reference to the parallels with massacre and slavery, 'so that we do not have to ask forgiveness one more time in the twenty-first century'.

For all Father Valeriano's defiance, the Roman Catholic Church has remained stuck fast in its opposition to condoms, and he has remained at work in São Paulo caring for the sick and orphaned of the Aids epidemic. These are the two faces that Roman Catholicism has presented to the world – one an expression of compassion and caring, the other a mask of rigid doctrine. I was in São Paulo three months after the accession of Pope Benedict. Father Valeriano told me he saw no likelihood of a relaxation in the Vatican view on condoms.

The only statement the new Pope had made on Aids at that point was to a group of South African bishops visiting Rome in June 2005. He deplored 'a breakdown in sexual morality' in Africa; he expressed great concern about Aids and prayed for 'the widows, orphans, [and] young mothers' affected by the epidemic; and he restated the Church's traditional teaching as being 'the only failsafe way to prevent the spread of HIV/Aids'.

In this Pope Benedict was following almost word for word the exhortation of his predecessor delivered a full decade earlier to the African bishops. John Paul II referred to 'the role played in the spread of this disease by irresponsible sexual behaviour' and spoke of the 'safeguard which chastity gives'. Pope Benedict's words were a little more elaborate, perhaps in acknowledgement of the hundreds of thousands who had sickened and died in the meantime through personal, political and religious disregard for sensible prevention strategies.

Cardinal Wojtyla became John Paul II in 1978, three years before the first Aids cases were reported in the United States. In November 1981 he appointed Cardinal Josef Ratzinger, the future Benedict XVI, to head the Congregation for the Doctrine of the Faith, once the office of the Inquisition. In doing so, in the very first year of Aids, the Pope cemented the central conservative partnership of his papacy and froze attitudes towards matters of sexual morality.

Pope John Paul never used the word condom in public, but he did speak of 'the essential evil of the contraceptive act'. Despite the enormity of the Aids disaster, he never reconsidered his opposition to one simple way to prevent infection and save life. When the United Nations staged its special session on Aids in 2001, it was again Cardinal Barragán who declared on the Vatican's behalf that it had 'in no way changed its moral position' on the 'use of condoms as a means of preventing HIV infection'.

Public discussion of the Vatican's position on condoms and Aids in the developing world remained surprisingly muted until the BBC television programme *Panorama* chose in 2003 to mark the twenty-fifth anniversary of Pope John Paul's accession with a film called *Sex and the Holy City*. It examined the human impact of the Pope's conservatism in the areas of abortion and contraception, and it devoted a final section to Aids.

In the programme the Roman Catholic Archbishop of Nairobi, Raphael Ndingi Mwana's Nzeki, responded to the Aids calamity in Kenya by saying that condoms were causing the spread of the disease because young people believed they were protected when they were not. He did not actually say that condoms should be banned, but he did state that no one should be using them. Tackled on a pamphlet produced by Kenya's Catholic bishops that claimed the Aids virus could pass through latex, Archbishop Nzeki said: 'We are not peddling ignorance. We shall be proved the only people who have been right in this matter in the long run.'

In an interview at the Vatican, the *Panorama* reporter Steve Bradshaw put the claim about HIV passing through latex to Cardinal Alfonso López Trujillo, the Colombian who heads the Pontifical Council for the Family and thus has principal responsibility for matters to do with sex and reproduction. The Cardinal was a close ally of Pope John Paul from early on in his papacy and is said to have been a key figure in facing down radical movements inside and outside the Church in Latin America.

Bradshaw: 'Is it the position of the Vatican that the virus, the HIV virus can pass through a condom?'

Cardinal Trujillo: 'Yes, yes, because this is something which the scientific community accepts, and doctors know what we are saying. You cannot talk about safe sex. One should speak of human value, about the family, and about fidelity.'

Bradshaw: 'But I have spoken to the World Health Organization and they say it is simply not true that the HIV virus can pass through latex from which condoms are made.'

Cardinal Trujillo: 'Well, they are wrong about that. No dialogue is possible at that level, scientifically speaking, because this is an easily recognizable fact.'

Cardinals in a hole should stop digging. Cardinal Trujillo was upset by the amount of attention his scientific assertion received around the world, and he might have responded with a dignified restatement of the Church's moral teachings. Unwisely he chose to try and justify his position on technical grounds. When I asked for an interview and was again turned down, his office sent me the twenty-page document which he issued as a rejoinder to the *Panorama* programme.

The document is entitled 'Family Values Versus Safe Sex' and is a thorough-going assault on condoms. As well as questioning their permeability, Cardinal Trujillo's paper says condom packets should have warning labels on them, like cigarettes, pointing out their failure rates. Safe sex campaigns are an 'invitation to promiscuity' and pressurize young people into having sex. The Cardinal's document refers darkly to 'certain economic interests on the part of condom producers', once again suggesting that the world's public health campaigners are somehow in the pocket of the condom manufacturers.

On the risks from condoms, the Cardinal's document conflates his original allegation that they let through the Aids virus with the broader question of their reliability. Manufacturing defects certainly account for some failures, as do poor storage and ignorance over how to use them. Sensible public health officials have never claimed that condoms guarantee 100 per cent protection, and they are now often under political and religious pressure to refer to 'safer sex' rather than 'safe sex' and 'correct and consistent condom use' rather than simply advising people to use them.

But the fact is that the sexually active, in particular those unsure of their partners' sexual health, are overwhelmingly safer using condoms than taking fright at the propaganda directed against them. Only those worried about condoms on religious or moral grounds insist on attaching health warnings to them, with the seemingly intentional purpose of discouraging people from using them in the first place.

Cardinal Trujillo's elaboration on the charge that condoms had holes in them was persuasively dismissed when *Panorama* returned to the subject with a film called *Can Condoms Kill?* On examination, the risk seemed to be somewhere between theoretical and negligible. Scientists from institutions whom the Cardinal had quoted denied the implications placed on their work. They included Dr Dave Lytle, a former senior research bio-physicist at the United States Food and Drug Administration who concluded: 'Latex condom is a very effective barrier. A few may allow minimal exposure, and if I were to give my children or grandchildren advice about whether to use condoms, I would say, "Absolutely!" '

The Church's uncompromising opposition to condoms has had its gravest impact in Africa. It is here, where the Aids crisis is at its worst, that the Church is at its most uniformly dogmatic and here also where it can expect the most unquestioning adherence from its followers. *Panorama*'s film concluded with the story of a Ugandan woman called Harriet Nakabugo who had married a man with Aids and feared that she was now HIV-positive herself. Her faith meant that she could not even ask her husband to use a condom. 'As Catholics we are not allowed to use them,' she said. 'They were designed for prostitutes. I would miss all of God's blessings and my reward would definitely be hell.'

The reporter Steve Bradshaw asked Cardinal Emmanuel Wamala, Archbishop of Kampala, about Harriet's case. He responded: 'Well, if it is wrong to use the condom, then her choice is the right one.'

'You're really saying that it could be better to die than to use a condom if that's your belief?'

'If that's one's belief, yes, it's better.'

'That's a harsh doctrine, isn't it?'

'Well, Christ's teaching has never been easy, has it?'

That lack of pity has condemned thousands to sickness and death. More than two in five marriages in Uganda are 'discordant', and the figures are similar in the generalized epidemics elsewhere in Africa. Time and time again it is uninfected younger women entering into marriage with older men who are most at risk.

The discordancy question has belatedly prompted more rigorous thinking from a few senior figures in the Church in Europe.

The clearest statement came in 2004 from the Belgian Cardinal Godfried Daneels who told an interviewer: 'If someone is HIV-positive and his partner says, "I want to have sexual relations with you," basically he should not do so. But if he does, then he must use a condom, otherwise he risks breaking the commandment, "Thou shalt not kill." '

Africa's own Catholic hierarchy has been shockingly unresponsive to the problem. When I travelled to Uganda in June 2005 there was a conference of East African bishops in progress 'responding to the challenges of HIV/Aids' with the admirable title 'Called to be a Good Samaritan'. There was discussion about discordancy and an item in the conference report devoted to 'Couples with Special Difficulties'. It would have been better if they had not bothered.

'As shepherds of the Catholic Church,' it began, 'we have listened attentively to the cries of our people living with HIV/Aids and they have many questions. But let us be honest, there are no easy answers and not because we do not want to give them but [because] they are simply not there. Let us not fall into the trap of feeling guilty or diminished when challenged by a worldly mentality that would like to solve all kinds of problems. When confronted with a situation like this let us turn to Christ and imitate Him in helping people find meaning for their suffering.'

This, surely, is one of the meanest responses to Aids ever recorded.

When the conference was over, one of the bishops was asked this question by Dr David Apuuli, head of Uganda's Aids commission: 'If a couple came to you, part of your flock, and said "My wife is negative and I am positive, what do you advise me to do?"' The Bishop laughed. 'Our hands are tied,' he said. 'We failed to resolve the issue. Our hands are tied, right from Rome.'

For a humane view of the Catholic dilemma over condoms in Africa, I was recommended to meet Father Michael Kelly in the Zambian capital Lusaka. Now in his mid-seventies, Father Michael is from County Offaly, in Ireland. He first came to Zambia for Jesuit training fifty years ago, and he has lived there without interruption for the past forty years. He is a citizen of Zambia and intends to die there.

Length of experience alone would mark Father Michael out as someone with a real knowledge of the country and its people. But there is more to him than that. In another life he might have been a theologian or perhaps a mathematician. In fact his doctorate is in child psychology and his professional career has taken him from school teacher to headmaster, and then from university lecturer to professor of education at the University of Zambia. It was his appreciation of what Aids might do to the education system that helped focus international attention on the broader social consequences of the epidemic.

'Unfortunately a lot of my projections have been realized,' Father Michael told me. Teachers have been hard hit by Aids, in large part because of their status in the community and what is called 'transactional sex' where poor girls trade their bodies for gifts or favours, even for better school marks. It was said to me in Zambia that the biggest Aids risk for a man is to have a job and the biggest risk for a woman is to get married. In the education field, it is not only the death of teachers and the dearth of replacements that have taken their toll. There is the prolonged sickness that precedes death, the teachers who can work only when they feel well enough, and the classes that are left untaught and unattended as a result. And just as Aids has undermined education systems in southern Africa, so too has it struck at health systems and, increasingly, through the death and sickness of able-bodied workers, at agricultural production.

Changing attitudes among young people in Zambia have given Father Michael grounds for optimism about the future. As in several other African countries, the figures for HIV infection among the young have come down sharply. 'They recognize the problem and know they have got to do something about it,' Father Michael said. 'There is much more of a sense of responsibility among young people than there was in the past.'

What of the role of condoms? Father Michael told me of an exchange he had had with Dr Waza Kaunda, son of the former Zambian president, who runs his father's charitable foundation and looks after Aids orphans. Father Michael told Dr Kaunda that he thought children should begin to receive information about condoms at around the age of 7. 'Oh no, Father, that's much too late!' was the reply. 'It should begin the day they start at pre-school.'

Father Michael candidly admitted to me that he would like to believe that condom promotion led to greater promiscuity, but he had examined the evidence and found that this was not the case. 'It may do so in one or two individuals, of course, but in a general sub-population it does not. It is leading to a delay in sex, to fewer pregnancies and to other beneficial outcomes.'

He also rejected the view of American abstinence campaigners that since condom promotion had failed to curb Aids in Africa, then something else should be tried instead. 'It never really took off in a way that it could be deemed a failure.' Abstinence was of course the answer for schoolchildren, and he did not believe in handing out condoms like sweets – 'because someone will suck a sweet eventually'. But any school Aids programme 'must have the condom element. We're failing them if we don't give them that information even though we're not promoting them. Even if we're not distributing them, they must have the information.'

What of the role of the Church? Father Michael is critical, but not primarily because of the Church's failure to promote condoms. Rather the reverse. 'The harm they have done is by opposing them,' he said. 'That is what I object to and what I don't like.

'One cannot take sides. We treasure our values, but that doesn't mean we have to condemn the values of others. Abstinence people are saying the condom people are fostering promiscuity. They are not! They're trying to work against the epidemic! Then the condom people say that abstinence is impossible. It is not! If people would not seek to undermine the position of the other, we would be much further forward in combating the epidemic.'

I asked Father Michael whether he thought the Church was culpable in the deaths from Aids. 'There was culpability, and I think there still is. We're not grappling with the problem with the seriousness it requires. I think lives would have been saved if the Vatican had been more accommodating towards the total ABC [Abstinence, Be Faithful, Condoms] approach.'

But how can Father Michael reconcile his acceptance of the role of condoms with the teachings of the Church? His answer was to advance two ecclesiastical principles. The first is that of double effect where the same action can have two outcomes, one good and one bad. Condom use prevents conception (bad) but also prevents the transmission of a fatal disease (good). 'Since the higher principle is the retaining of life, then that takes precedence.' The second, related principle is that of the lesser evil. If a person is determined to do something wrong, he can be advised not to do something else at the same time that compounds the offence. 'Having sex outside marriage is morally wrong,' said Father Michael. 'Don't aggravate it by transmitting a sickness at the same time. The lesser of the two evils is to take steps to avoid transmitting a disease.'

It was through Father Michael that I visited the Mothers of Mercy hospice at Chilanga, on the outskirts of Lusaka, and witnessed the death of 37-year-old Esther Kamusa with which I began this book. The guiding principle of mercy, which was on such eloquent display there, has not always been so evident in the Church's response to Aids. Some churchmen have even attacked the aid-givers if they failed to subscribe rigorously enough to conventional Catholic teaching on condoms.

The British organization Cafod (Catholic Agency for Overseas Development) has been engaged in the response to Aids in Africa since the disease was first identified in Uganda in the 1980s. Cafod still works in the Rakai district where the Ugandan crisis began. In the early years it was quite possible to concentrate on the traditional caring role of the Church, leaving the thornier matter of prevention to others. Cafod is overseen by the bishops of England and Wales and so must respect the Church's opposition to contraception and condoms. But as the Aids epidemic progressed from tragedy to developmental catastrophe, it became increasingly difficult to maintain such distinctions, particularly when working with local Catholic communities witnessing widespread death and illness from the disease.

In 2001 Cafod drew up a statement saying that it did not fund the supply, distribution or promotion of condoms. But it said two other things as well – that individuals should be given 'full information about all means of HIV prevention' and that Cafod would not support programmes 'that give false or misleading information about prevention'. It gave two examples of such misinformation as 'HIV will inevitably pass through holes in latex; or that condoms contain HIV'. Despite fears within Cafod that even the mention of condoms would upset supporters in the parishes, the roof did not cave in.

In 2004 the agency decided to give further expression to its experience of Aids prevention, first in a paper to an international conference in Bangkok and then in an article written by Dr Ann Smith, the agency's Aids strategist, for the Catholic weekly *The Tablet.* 'The data is clear that condoms, when used correctly and consistently, reduce but do not completely remove the risk of HIV infection,' Dr Smith wrote. 'This fact cannot be excluded from or misrepresented in any information on risk reduction strategies, regardless of the political or moral position of those promoting them.' In sentiment and approach, this formulation was almost identical to the 2001 statement. But three years had elapsed and by now US abstinence campaigners had changed the terms of the Aids prevention debate. Headlines declared 'Catholic charity defies Pope with condom support' (*The Times*) and 'Catholics back Aids condoms' (*The Daily Telegraph*), and this time the roof did begin to fall in.

Two small Christian groups – Christian Order and Catholic Action Group – took aim. Christian Order wrote a thirty-page 'exposé' of Cafod which it said it distributed to 10,000 people. The headline was 'Contributing to Cafod is a Sin!' An abridged version of this article was then produced and a further 70,000 distributed. The Catholic Action Group demanded that Cafod make a statement saying that it did not 'condone the use of condoms in any circumstances' by the end of January 2005 or face a funding boycott. There was a flow of rather menacing emails and telephone calls to the agency and to the parishes saying that the clock was ticking.

In the event, a few parishes did withhold funding and there were a number of protest letters. There were also many letters of support. More significant than reaction at a local level was the fact that this public argument had put the bishops on the spot. Discussions began over a form of words on condoms to which both the bishops and the development agency could subscribe. If the bishops had formally disavowed the agency's careful formulations on the role of condoms in Aids prevention up to that point, there would have been at least one senior resignation at the agency. The statement that emerged did refer to Cafod's commitment to scientifically correct information, but the emphasis had perceptibly shifted. In stating that the agency 'neither funds nor advocates the supply, distribution or promotion of condoms' it came very close to, but just stopped short of, saying that it did not believe they should be used.

The new Cafod statement received the backing of the English and Welsh bishops who said it was 'in conformity with Catholic moral teaching'. In early 2005 it was taken to Rome and discussed with Cardinal Lozano Barragán who expressed no concerns about the wording. It was also shown to Cardinal Trujillo who similarly raised no objections. The chapter is now closed, until tension between church prohibition and developmental imperatives arises again.

In the broader church, there was no thaw in Pope Benedict's stance on condoms during the first year of his papacy. At that point, with the 25th anniversary of the epidemic approaching, there were signs that the glacier might be starting to melt. After a flurry of interest over yet another Cardinal (this time Cardinal Carlo Maria Martini, the 79-year-old former Archbishop of Milan who is thought to have been the runner-up to Benedict in 2005) endorsing the principle of the lesser evil in the case of married couples where one partner has the virus, the Vatican announced that it was now studying the issue with a view to making a fresh pronouncement on the condom question.

Cardinal Barragán himself, with his responsibilities for healthcare, had been charged with conducting the study and was involving scientists and theologians. It was clear that any liberalisation here would be limited to married 'discordant' couples, but it seemed possible that the Vatican was setting off down the same slippery slope that for a quarter of a century it had refused even to place a foot. If it became acceptable for married Christians to protect their spouses and to save life, were other Catholic sinners simply to be condemned to death and damnation? It was the question posed so eloquently by Father Valeriano, the parish priest in São Paulo who said that Christ came to earth so that everyone should have life, and then criticised his church for failing to accept the fragility of human beings. It may well be, as he also told me, that the Vatican will one day have to apologise for its role in the Aids epidemic of the twentieth century just as it finally apologised for its sins in colonial Brazil five hundred years earlier.

8

The Lost Decade

'The wages of sin unfortunately are well-known.
The wages of sin are death.'
Former President Frederick Chiluba of Zambia

Frederick Chiluba agreed to meet me at his bungalow in Lusaka, and we conducted our interview by the swimming pool in his garden. 'It's not Robben Island,' said Zambia's former president, referring to Nelson Mandela's apartheid prison, 'but it is a form of house arrest.' Mr Chiluba had been in court that morning for a hearing on corruption charges. The sums involved had been scaled down from the hundreds of millions of dollars he was originally accused of embezzling, but the authorities had confiscated his passport and he could not travel.

Mr Chiluba was President from 1991 to 2002, the decade in which HIV infections in Zambia grew to their current proportions of about one in six of the adult population. The record shows that the President was regularly reminded of the need for strong national leadership in the battle to contain the epidemic. His personal response in this area is generally regarded as poor.

In 1999 Zambia staged the eleventh international conference on Aids in Africa which President Chiluba was due to open. He did not turn up. I asked him why. He said he had other engagements that week, and then offered this: 'I accept the criticism fully, because people did not understand my philosophy. I wanted the government, not Chiluba, to be credited with the success of that conference.'

A pre-conference meeting of African leaders had to be cancelled because none of the fifteen other heads of government invited had turned up either. Dr Peter Piot, head of UNAIDS, made an appointment to see Mr Chiluba to talk about the extent of the Aids crisis in Zambia. He received instead a lecture on the impact of malaria.

Stephen Lewis, the UN Secretary-General's special representative for Aids in Africa, observed a year after Chiluba left office that Zambia was now 'emerging from the bleak and dark ages of denial into the light of recognition. The bitter truth is that in the regime of the previous president, nothing was done. He spent his time disavowing the reality of Aids, and hurling obstacles in the way of those who were desperate to confront the epidemic.' Mr Lewis recalled attending an African summit 'and sitting down with the then President Chiluba, and asking him what he intended to do about Aids, and he simply wouldn't talk to me about it'.

In our interview by the pool, Mr Chiluba accepted that his country had 'lost an army of Zambians' to Aids and that there had been 'quite a few lapses along the way'. But he seemed largely disengaged from the detail of the crisis, resorting to the pieties that politicians voice when they have nothing very concrete to say. At one stage he said: 'The mission was to create a national leadership that would harness every available force and effort to fight Aids.'

There were indeed Zambian ministers and officials who worked hard in response to the Aids crisis, but no one I spoke to in Lusaka recalled any such leadership from the top during Mr Chiluba's decade in power.

Where the former president was more engaged was in a fierce and fundamental Christian perspective on the disease. He accepted that he was himself a sinner and that strong ideas about sin had contributed to keeping his country in denial over the Aids crisis, but he added: 'The wages of sin unfortunately are well-known. The wages of sin are death.'

Frederick Chiluba was born and brought up in the Church of Scotland, but was 'born again' soon after serving a prison spell for trades union activities in 1981. His new conversion happened on a visit to neighbouring Malawi where he asked members of a German evangelical mission to 'lay hands' on him and where he then 'spoke in tongues'. As president he would sometimes preach at one of Lusaka's rapidly growing evangelical churches. He also proclaimed Zambia a Christian nation, a status confirmed in a new constitution.

As so often in the faltering international efforts to counter Aids, it was attitudes towards the condom that were Mr Chiluba's moral touchstone. 'I believe that condoms are a way of encouraging sin. It is like saying "Let me sin, God will not punish me because I have a cover [he gestured at his lap], so let me go and sin."

'I am surprised that the churches talk about the condom. They should be the last people ever to talk about the condom. If we were all observing abstinence, the rule of abstention and the rule of prevention can work.'

Mr Chiluba said that he aligned himself fully with Pope John Paul II and President George W. Bush in their attitudes towards

Aids and how to prevent it. 'I am not a Catholic, but I followed the late John Paul II in his response to Aids. I read him. I kissed every article he wrote because he stood on the truth.'

Of George W. Bush and the new US emphasis on abstinence, Mr Chiluba said: 'Do you wonder why he won the election? He was following God's leadership and guidance. He won because he received God's instruction and relayed it to the American people. I support George Bush a million times!'

The first case of Aids in Zambia was diagnosed in 1984 and the epidemic grew virtually unchecked through that decade. In 1985, 8 per cent of young women attending Lusaka ante-natal clinics were testing HIV-positive. In 1987 the figure rose to 11 per cent. At the start of the 1990s, it stood at more than 20 per cent and stayed there.

In a publicly Christian country responding with discomfort and denial to a sexually transmitted disease, one death alone promised for a time to shake national complacency. Dr Kenneth Kaunda, Zambia's first president and one of Africa's great independence leaders, told me that he was chairing a meeting of the anti-apartheid Front Line States when he was called to his son's bedside. Masuzyo Kaunda, a 30-year-old businessman, had fallen seriously ill at his home on Zambia's Copperbelt and had been brought to State House in Lusaka for medical treatment. He died of Aids two days before Christmas in 1986. Dr Kaunda talked to his wife Betty and they decided on the brave course of a press conference to publicize the cause of Masuzyo's death.

'It was a painful thing to do, but unless we fight this wild animal called HIV/Aids in this way, we have no chance of fighting it effectively.'

Dr Kaunda took another step in his personal crusade when he became the first African leader to be tested publicly for the Aids virus. 'I was tested and found negative,' he told me, and added: 'Even if I had been found positive, I would have gone ahead and told the world I was positive. Then I would have been fighting Aids being positive myself.'

Like almost every other family in Zambia, Dr and Mrs Kaunda have suffered great personal loss through the Aids crisis. He began to count for me how many close relatives had died of the disease. He stopped at five. They included grandchildren and nieces. The Kaundas have directly experienced Africa's orphan crisis through looking after Masuzyo's children – who now have children of their own. Their daughter-in-law, Masuzyo's wife, is HIV-positive and lives in London for easier access to treatment.

Dr Kaunda's personal testimony might have launched the robust national Aids programme that Zambia needed, but it did not. Individuals like the Jesuit Father Michael Kelly told me how he had been inspired by Kaunda's stance to tackle the impact of the disease in the field of education, but social and religious conservatism outweighed the impact of the President's initiative. When the Zambians threw Kaunda out of office in the 1991 elections, the national response to Aids stalled further.

Through the work of his Aids foundation, Dr Kaunda has recently focused his energy on the children of the epidemic, but he has also advanced a common-sense approach to prevention. He is the son of a Church of Scotland missionary and a man of faith himself, but his Christian credentials were seriously questioned when he began to argue openly for condoms.

'When I said this I was attacked by some church leaders. I had become an evil man. I pretended to be a Christian, and now I was teaching people how to misbehave. My reply was "Dear friends, thank you for what you're saying, but remember this: among those we have lost are Reverends, Priests, Fathers, Sisters and many others in church work. If you had not preached against the use of condoms, those people might have been alive today. Now they're six feet down and you can't help them. If they'd used condoms, they might have been alive, and you would have been able to help them spiritually to recover." '

Kenneth Kaunda's support for condoms has put him at odds with the new and expanding evangelical churches. These churches have ties with the American evangelical movement and can expect to benefit from the US government's emphasis on abstinence and fidelity in preference to condoms. According to figures from the US embassy in Lusaka, more than $4 million was spent promoting abstinence and fidelity in Zambia in 2004, much less than on condom distribution and services for 'high risk' groups. In 2005 the abstinence and fidelity budget was set to increase by 25 per cent, five times the increase allowed for the condom programmes.

The United States was prepared to fund condoms for groups like soldiers, truck drivers and prostitutes, but there was to be no emphasis on safe sex for the population at large. When I visited Zambia in the summer of 2005, the last television advertisements promoting condoms had come off the air a full year earlier, at exactly the time that money from the Bush Aids programme began to flow. There were no further plans to use the mass media to tell young people about protection through condoms. After years of growth there were signs that condom usage was beginning to decline.

The move away from condom promotion for young Zambians flew in the face of evidence which had emerged from one of the country's most successful mass media campaigns. It was known as HEART, or Helping Each Other Act Responsibly Together and was aimed at 13- to 19-year-olds. It was American-funded, but conceived and executed before the era of George W. Bush. What was unusual about it was that it set out to give young people apparently contradictory advice on the merits of abstinence and condom use at the same time. Each TV advertisement ended with the line 'Abstain or Use a Condom Every Time'.

Conventional wisdom suggested that young people would end up confused and take no notice of either message. The new politics of Aids demanded that A for Abstinence needed to be rigorously separated out from C for Condoms. But far from being confused, young Zambians ended up paying proper attention to both messages. As common sense might have suggested, some young people did one thing and others did another. According to evaluations published in 2001, around three-quarters of those who had seen the campaign began talking about the subject of Aids, abstinence and condoms. Almost 30 per cent of them said they had adopted abstinence as a result of the campaign and 15 per cent said they had started using condoms.

It seemed an endorsement of the position of former President Kaunda who had participated in the HEART television campaigns himself. 'Abstinence and condoms have to be coupled,' he told me. 'We have no choice in the matter.' He added that schoolchildren needed to be encouraged to abstain but 'if you can't abstain, use condoms!'

Even during the successful HEART campaign, objections from the churches and others succeeded in having all the condom advertisements taken off the air. One of them remained permanently banned. This showed young Zambian women talking about whether they should allow their boyfriends to have unprotected sex. 'No Condom, No Sex' was their conclusion. As well as outraging the moralists, it also offended the conservatives for whom young women should neither be discussing sex nor deciding how men should behave.

Aids campaigners in Zambia continued to promote condoms on TV until the US changed its prevention strategy under the Bush programme. The alliance between American and Zambian conservatives appeared to rule out such ventures in future.

'I know the churches that supported President Bush in his campaign are very powerful in their stand against condoms,' said Dr Kaunda. 'But whatever other people may say, I am saying "Have we reached that stage of purity in our lives?" The answer is no!

'The attitude of the new churches worries me. If we can get everybody in this country to respond to our call "Prevention is better than cure, so abstain" then all is well, there is no problem. But if we abstained, why are millions dying and why are millions suffering? We are failing, and pretending we're pure.'

The new churches in Zambia are most fluently represented by Bishop Joshua Banda, of the Pentecostal Assemblies of God. As I waited for him at his church office in Lusaka, a 4 x 4 vehicle drove into the compound with an 'Africa for Jesus' sticker on the windscreen. When the Bishop himself arrived, he was in a sharp suit, waistcoat and tie, and wore smart rimless glasses. He spoke of the 'competitive advantage' that his church enjoyed in tackling Aids. This was because of the strength of its moral teaching aimed at abstinence for young people and fidelity for the married. He said he was not opposed to condoms in all circumstances, but they had been far too heavily promoted in the past and his church would never distribute them.

Bishop Banda claimed that condom promotion was too tied in with commercial interests. 'Condom social marketing has always been financially very strongly backed,' he said. 'This is an attempt to promote the belief that young people will not abstain. But we are making assumptions here. We have not had a way of putting as much weight on abstinence and being faithful as on condoms because we have believed too much in condoms.'

Bishop Banda's Assembly of God Church is the official representative in Lusaka of the Children's Aids Fund in Washington. This is the organization run by Anita and Shepherd Smith with close links to the Bush White House. Because of its association with Mrs Janet Museveni, the born-again wife of the President of Uganda, the Children's Aids Fund was controversially provided with USAID funds despite having its original application rejected.

Through the Children's Aids Fund, Bishop Banda was hoping to receive US funding for an Aids treatment centre in Lusaka where HIV-positive people would come for their antiretroviral drugs. The Pentecostalists would also like to expand their work with street children and prostitutes. In the competition that exists between the churches in Zambia, a senior Protestant in Lusaka told me that the Pentecostalists had only recently come into the Aids field and argued that their interest owed as much to the availability of US funds as to Christian charity. The same senior Protestant also acknowledged that 'it was the Catholics who were doing all the work' and that even mainstream Protestant churches had been slow to respond to Aids.

One afternoon at Bishop Banda's Assembly of God Church in Lusaka I attended a meeting of the prostitutes whom the church was trying to save. Fifty young women were sitting in the pews. 'We teach them the word of God and we teach them skills,' Bishop Banda told me. The project is called 'Operation Paseli' after the street on which the church stands. It started when a group of young churchgoers emerged at the end of an all-night prayer meeting to find a prostitute and her client having sex on the pavement.

'Look, there's no way we can let this continue,' Bishop Banda told his congregation. He cancelled the evening service and his worshippers went out to meet the prostitutes. 'We began talking to them about alternatives. "If we pulled you off the streets and gave you something to do, would you be ready to come?" and they said yes.' Eighty women had so far completed courses in sewing and dress-making, and another eighty were ready to graduate.

I spoke to four of the young women – Jane, Sarah, Priscilla and Marjorie. All had started working the streets as teenagers, Marjorie at the age of 13. Two of them were still in their teens. Jane's story was typical. She was 17, and had been working as a prostitute since leaving school the year before. There was simply no alternative if she wanted to feed herself. Her father had died of tuberculosis – which probably meant undiagnosed Aids – and so had her two older sisters. They had both done the same as Jane – left school and gone on the streets. They had worked for a few years as prostitutes, become infected, sickened and died. Jane had heard of the church project through a friend and she was really enjoying it. There was a chance that things would work out better for Jane than they had for her two sisters, but it was only a very slim one. 'The problem continues to be hunger,' Jane said.

Helping prostitutes to lead other lives is important work. So too is working with prostitutes to make sure their health is protected. Abstinence and fidelity messages will hardly be enough on their own, yet it is those on which Bishop Banda and the Pentecostalists want to concentrate. He said he was planning to conduct a detailed study into the relative effects of abstinence and fidelity campaigning compared to condoms. He was confident of what he would find and distrusted the 'comprehensive' approach to Aids. 'That argument has intent,' he told me. 'The intent is to get everybody at a place where they're distributing condoms.'

Washington's policy shift and the massive funds which underwrite it have tipped Zambia's national discussion in favour of those who believe there is a better approach to preventing Aids than promoting condoms. Former President Kaunda's plea that condoms should play the central role in prevention has been set aside. There is some evidence from the countryside that Zambians have already got the message that condoms are not reliable and should only be used by 'high-risk', that is 'immoral', people.

Zambia will be a key test for the new US global Aids strategy. In its first annual report published in March 2005, the Bush emergency plan announced that it had so far reached more than 40 million people around the world with abstinence programmes and a further 140 million with programmes combining abstinence and faithfulness. There were as yet no hard figures on progress towards the target of 7 million HIV infections prevented by 2008. Stopping all those infections, doing that arithmetic, and persuading the world that the sums add up, were the biggest challenges facing US Aids administrators.

A remarkable insight into the impact of the Bush prevention strategy where it mattered most was provided by a report produced in Washington in April 2006 by the Government Accountability Office, the audit and evaluation arm of Congress. The GAO was set the task of investigating the effects of abstinence spending on American Aids programmes in the countries worst-affected by the epidemic. GAO investigators had the advantage denied to journalists of unfettered access to US aid officials in the field, and were further able to guarantee the candour and validity of their findings by agreeing not to name the officials they interviewed or even identify the missions for which they worked. The GAO underlined the scale of the US commitment to abstinence and fidelity by reporting that for every one dollar now being spent on condoms, two dollars were going on abstinence.

The report presented a troubling picture of an Aids programme in which officials on the ground were being prevented by Washington's restrictions from using their own professional judgement to respond flexibly to local epidemics. They were having to ignore other priorities in order to satisfy the drive for abstinence. This process went beyond the downplaying of condoms. Three US country teams told the GAO that they would be forced to cut services to pregnant HIV-positive women at risk of passing the infection to their babies – an important priority for the Bush programme and straightforwardly achieved with drugs – and one team said that it had already made such cuts. Another team said that it would have to scale back projects aimed at reducing HIV acquired in hospitals and clinics through contaminated blood supplies and medical equipment. Yet another reported that it would have to cut back on its care programmes for Aids patients.

The GAO also dealt with the vexed question of how the Bush programme intended to produce persuasive calculations to show that it had reached the seven-million prevention target. In their second report to Congress in February 2006, US Aids officials said that the United States Census Bureau was now at work on statistics comparing what would have happened to HIV infection rates in the 15 focus countries with what actually happened as a result of US interventions. The first figures will be published in 2007. Only by 2010, with the evidence in and the calculations done, will it become clear whether or not the Bush plan has truly turned the tide of the global epidemic, as the President promised.

The GAO report provided its own startling account of how the Bush programme would produce these figures and how the US Census Bureau, not widely known for its work outside the country, came to take charge of the process. Originally, said the

GAO, the Census Bureau was given the task of chairing a group to come up with the best means of evaluating progress towards the seven million. From early on, it was plain that the likeliest agency to get this crucial commission was the independent, privately owned Futures Group, which had an extensive background in public health consultancy in the developing world. The Futures Group was already at work in the field of Aids and had evolved methods of calculating infections averted and then attributing them to specific interventions. Their experience appeared tailor-made for the task in prospect. Indeed the Futures Group conducted just such an exercise on the first year of the Bush Aids programme in which it estimated that more than 500,000 infections might be prevented, but concluded that this would be achieved primarily though condom promotion and greater access to HIV testing rather than through the promotion of abstinence and fidelity. Unsurprisingly perhaps, the Futures Group did not get the commission. The US Census Bureau would do the job itself.

It further emerged that the Bush programme was not even now expecting its evaluators to establish whether prevented infections could be attributed to particular interventions. So after spending more than one billion dollars on abstinence-only promotion in the poor world over five years, US taxpayers will have no means of knowing whether their money has been well spent or not. Those who took the decision to go with the broad-sweep approach of the Government's Census Bureau in preference to more detailed analysis from the Futures Group argued that studies on the effects of abstinence promotion were scarce and unreliable. To critics of the Bush programme, that simply underlined the shaky basis of its decision in the first place to put so much faith in abstinence as the best way of reversing the tidal wave of Aids.

9

Crusaids against Prostitution

'Like shit from a bandit's horse.'

Gabriela Leite on the status of Brazilian sex workers

I visited the prostitutes of Rio de Janeiro on the same day as Dr Peter Piot, executive director of UNAIDS. He called on them in the middle of the day, and I spent the evening with them. Dr Piot was in Rio to attend an international Aids conference. I was there to understand the success that Brazil has had in containing Aids. Because prostitutes have a lot of sex, much of it with men who do not care about their own or their women's health, they are at great risk of acquiring HIV and spreading it, and that makes them a very important group in tackling the epidemic.

Dr Piot and I both wanted to see the same woman. Her name is Gabriela Leite and she runs a prostitutes' welfare organization called Davida – 'For Life'. She also holds office in a number of Brazilian and international prostitution networks. Gabriela is a petite, animated woman in her early fifties who worked for upwards of twenty years as a prostitute. She would probably have been an agitator in any walk of life, but a determination to campaign and organize made her unusual in a job which most prefer to keep quiet.

Gabriela was working in São Paulo in the late 1970s when city police conducted one of their periodic and crude crackdowns on the sex trade. The women were forced off the streets and had to defy police orders in order to tout for custom. Two of Gabriela's friends were arrested. One, who was pregnant, died in custody; the other simply 'disappeared'. Gabriela told the other girls that they must protest, but the girls replied: 'We can't do that. We're prostitutes.'

But they did protest, and at a time when there was agitation in the air against Brazil's long dictatorship. They received welcome support from São Paulo's actors. Gabriela was lent a theatre for the evening and 3,000 people turned up to denounce police brutality. The local police chief was transferred. It was a great victory. Gabriela had found her twin vocations – prostitution and agitation. 'If we can achieve this, we can achieve other things,' Gabriela told the girls. 'We don't want to fight for anything else,' the girls replied. 'We're prostitutes.'

After that Gabriela travelled the country as a hooker and a hitch-hiker. 'Truck drivers are the sex workers' best friends,' she told me. In 1982 she arrived in Rio de Janeiro, which has the most open prostitution in the country. She has been a campaigner for prostitutes' rights ever since, and the Aids crisis has propelled her from the national to the international stage. On the front page of the June 2005 edition of Davida's magazine, there is a group photograph of Aids dignitaries and activists at the UN in New York. Included in the line-up are Kofi Annan, the Secretary-General, Dr Peter Piot from UNAIDS and Gabriela Leite.

I met Gabriela at a hookers' bar in the deep downtown of Rio. We sat on one side of the street drinking beer and conducting an interview while a carnival of short skirts, tight blouses, provocative dancing and a great deal of business passed by on the other side of the street. Our first topic was condoms. Was it true there was a shortage? Yes, she said, the authorities were supposed to deliver 20,000 a month, and only 1,500 had arrived. It was outrageous. The problem was the poor quality of imported condoms and a government decision to withdraw them. I marvelled once again at the level of international sophistication directed at Aids and the world's simultaneous incapacity to provide even the first and crudest line of defence against the disease.

Brazil has had a strong record on condom promotion despite the influence of the Roman Catholic Church. Early on in the Aids epidemic, in 1985, Brazilians were using about 5 million condoms a year. That rose to 700 million in 2003, and Dr Pedro Chequer, head of the country's National Aids Programme, told me he would like to drive it to 3 billion by 2008. One hundred million of them will be produced in a factory built deep in the Amazon jungle to honour Chico Mendes, the forest workers' leader who fought for the rights of local rubber tappers and was murdered by landowners in 1988.

Corresponding official efforts have been made to engage prostitutes in the struggle against Aids. Instead of pressing them to the margins as disease-carriers, moral delinquents or economic victims, they have been brought into the mainstream of the campaign. Prostitution is not illegal in Brazil – although pimping and living off immoral earnings are – and sex work is a recognized job description. Dr Chequer takes things a step further: 'At the National Aids Programme, it is part of our task to advocate the legalization of prostitution. They are our partners, they are part of our community. They are very important because we believe in peer education. It's not just women taking care of their own health, but spreading the word.'

'Shame-less Maria' is a good example of this approach. She was the cartoon heroine who spearheaded a recent government publicity campaign directed at prostitutes. 'Maria' is a saucer-eyed redhead who stared out from the covers of health booklets and lavatory walls. 'Don't be ashamed, my girl,' was the key message. 'You have a profession.' 'Don't be ashamed to be a prostitute; or to fight for your rights; or to use condoms.'

These efforts have worked. HIV prevalence among commercial sex workers in Brazil fell from 17.8 per cent in 1996 to 6.4 per cent in 2000 and has stayed at this level.

For Gabriela Leite, it is all to do with respect. If prostitutes are to be trusted to care for their own health and that of others, they have to be seen as more than the lowest of the low, more than 'shit from a bandit's horse', to use her own vivid Brazilian expression. In her view, prostitutes have to have rights as employees, and prostitution needs to be developed and controlled like any other business. Above all prostitutes are more than just victims, she told me.

Gabriela's views and the backing they received from the National Aids Programme drove Brazil into open dispute with the United States. Not only does the US government disapprove of prostitution – an unexceptional enough position to take – it also wants actively to diminish and preferably abolish it. This ambition is not wholly consistent with the position at home where, for instance, prostitution is legal in certain counties in Nevada. But this is now America's formal world view, backed by the authority of the US Congress.

When legislation authorizing the Bush Aids programme was passing through Congress in 2003, Representative Chris Smith of New Jersey promoted an amendment denying US funds to any organization which did not have a policy 'explicitly opposing prostitution and sex trafficking'. Chris Smith had already promoted an Act against sex trafficking, but in drawing no real distinction between that gross crime and the phenomenon of prostitution he ended up doing a disservice to many women.

It took USAID lawyers two years to convert Congressman Smith's amendment into the basis of a binding contract on recipients of American assistance for the Aids programme. 'The US government is opposed to prostitution and related activities, which are inherently harmful and dehumanising, and contribute to the phenomenon of trafficking in persons,' said the document, appearing to give as great a priority to bearing down on prostitution as on trafficking. 'None of the funds made available under this agreement may be used to promote or advocate the legalisation or practice of prostitution or sex trafficking.'

The US demand for compliance with this new morality was conveyed to Brazil in late 2004 during discussions over the continuation of American-funded projects directed at such priority Aids groups as prostitutes, drug-takers and homosexuals. At one point in the negotiations, US officials tried to get Brazil to pursue some serious campaigning in favour of sexual abstinence, but the Brazilians were having none of that. The real sticking-point, however, was prostitutes' rights, and neither side would give an inch. There was $48 million at stake, about half of it already spent. The Americans insisted that if the Brazilians wanted the rest they would have to agree to move the goal posts – right in the middle of the game.

Brazil refused. Not only that. The government staged elaborate consultations between prostitutes' organizations and the National Aids Programme. Each publicly supported the other in rejecting American pressure. 'We will not sell ourselves,' Gabriela Leite told me, 'the American money is not welcome.' At an international Aids conference in Rio de Janeiro in July 2005, with senior US Aids officials in attendance, Dr Pedro Chequer said that Brazil's approach to Aids prevention was based on the evidence of what actually worked. 'Other approaches, such as those based on religious or other non-scientific considerations, will only serve to increase the spread and negative impact of the epidemic.'

The foundations of Brazil's success in combating Aids were laid in the 1980s as the country began to shake off years of military-backed dictatorship. There was nothing accidental in this connection. A free health system on the European model had been a basic objective of the democracy movement, and the new constitution of 1988 declared health care to be a social right. The Aids crisis was building at the same time, and became an early test of this political resolve. In so many other countries, the political response to Aids has been one of shame and neglect. In Brazil it became a defining challenge for democracy.

Brazil's new health system was put in place in 1990, and the following year Aids patients started receiving antiretroviral drugs and other medicines free of charge. When the life-prolonging ARV cocktails became available in the mid-1990s, they too were distributed free. A decade later there was international recognition of the quality of Brazil's achievement, but their Aids ambitions had not always been endorsed. United Nations agencies were wary of Brazil's promise of universal access to Aids treatment, with the international financial institutions believing that developing countries should not assume such social burdens. They have been proved wrong.

Brazil's Aids statistics make impressive reading. Patients are living longer. In 1989 they survived on average for five months after diagnosis. In 2002, they were surviving for almost five years. The death rate has come down sharply. Between 1996 and 2002 it fell by 50 per cent, which meant that 90,000 people survived who would otherwise have died. There was also a 70 per cent fall in all the other diseases associated with Aids and a reduction in hospital admissions of 80 per cent. As a consequence there were big savings in the health budget. In 2005 Brazil calculated that it had saved $1.23 billion in hospital and outpatient costs.

But the economics of saving people from dying of Aids are not that straightforward. The more Brazilians who survive, and the longer they do so, the more expensive it becomes for a government committed to treating them for nothing. Again the figures are remarkable. In the early years of Brazil's antiretroviral programme, about half the drugs budget was spent on local production in government-run pharmaceutical factories. That changed as intellectual property rules were tightened and international patents were more rigorously enforced. By 2004 four-fifths of the Aids programme's drugs budget was being spent on expensive imports.

This situation is set to get worse. Brazil spent $259 million in 2004 on antiretrovirals. That figure was to rise to $416 million for 2005, and still further in subsequent years. New generations of drugs will be required to keep Brazilians alive and more will need them for longer. The import bill will be driven ever higher. 'This is not sustainable,' Dr Pedro Chequer of the National Aids Programme told me flatly. 'The only option we have right now to have a sustainable Aids programme is to use the TRIPS agreement [the international arrangement enabling countries to set aside patent rules in public health emergencies] and our national law for local production. That's it. There is no other option.'

The implicit threat in this statement is that Brazil will issue compulsory licences for one or more of the drugs it needs for its Aids programme. Under world trade rules it may be morally and legally entitled to do so, but such a step would deeply antagonize the drugs companies and the US trade establishment. Countries think more than twice before provoking the wrath of the world trade superpower.

The United States once launched a complaint against Brazil at the World Trade Organization simply for having a law on the statute book allowing it to compel local pharmaceutical production. That case was one of the final acts of the Clinton presidency. It was quietly dropped by George W. Bush when the United Nations was on the point of staging a grand session on the Aids epidemic in New York in 2001.

During that momentous year of 2001 when the political and commercial dimensions of the Aids crisis began to become apparent, Brazil played a leading role in promoting the rights of developing countries to secure access to affordable medicines for their sick and dying. Many in Brazil, from committed bureaucrats to campaigning activists, continued to press the government to issue compulsory licences. The political price to be paid – and the likelihood of US trade sanctions – always dragged Brazilian ministers back from the brink. The ministers in turn were regularly and publicly branded as 'toothless tigers', roaring their determination to issue these licences at one moment and then thinking rather better of it the next.

The most acute tussle between Brazil and Big Pharma was played out over an Aids drug called Kaletra, manufactured by the American company Abbott Laboratories. Brazil's Minister of Health, Dr Humberto Costa, chose the eve of World Aids Day in 2004 to announce that he was going to issue a number of compulsory licences on imported antiretrovirals, including Kaletra. Then the haggling began.

At the time Brazilian doctors were prescribing Kaletra to 23,000 patients. It was costing the government around $60 million a year and the bill would keep going up as more and more HIV-positive people needed the drug. Brazilian officials reckoned they could save two-thirds of the $60 million if they manufactured Kaletra themselves.

Abbott was charging Brazil the equivalent of $1.17 per pill and the government was prepared to offer no more than 68 cents. After months of bargaining a deal was struck at the beginning of July 2005. Instead of $1.17 per pill, Abbott would charge the government 99 cents in 2006 and then on a sliding scale down to 70 cents by 2010 as the patent came closer to expiry. It seemed a reasonable compromise, but on the day the deal was announced the Minister, Dr Costa, was removed from office (nothing to do with the pharmaceutical argument, I was assured) and his successor insisted on tearing up the agreement and starting the whole process again.

Those who argued for compulsory licences were delighted that Dr Costa's agreement was being scrapped. He had not been tough enough. Even his civil servants said so. For the record, Dr Pedro Chequer, the country's senior Aids official, told me: 'We are lucky we have a new minister. We didn't agree with the negotiations or the conclusions.'

For Dr Chequer, local production is still the only solution and compulsory licensing is the only realistic approach. The alternative would be the sort of fudge reached with Abbott where the price was still about twice as much as it would have been had the patent been broken and the drugs manufactured in Brazil. 'The price of this agreement is to maintain Brazil as a backyard, just a consumer,' he told me.

Under Brazil's new Minister of Health, Saraiva Felipe, negotiations started up again. Not content with a price reduction from $1.17 to 99 cents, Felipe wanted it driven down towards the 41 cents per pill that represented the locally manufactured cost. At an international Aids conference, with Big Pharma executives listening, the Minister spoke harshly of 'abusive profits regimes' that worked against developing countries and added: 'I believe that questions of public health do indeed take precedence over the extortionate interests of the drugs industry.'

The rhetoric never quite matched the reality of Brazil's position – a need to balance its health budget against its larger trading interests. The haggling that began again in July was concluded in October 2005. The final deal provided for a price of 63 cents for Kaletra from 2006. It went some way towards meeting Brazil's health budget problems, but it did not solve them. It was a further advertisement, if one was needed, that the health interests of developing countries needed a more refined international response than crude haggling between governments and companies.

The division between Brazil and the United States over drugs prices was on vivid display when Dr Robert Gallo, the American scientist and controversial co-discoverer of the Aids virus, came to Brazil at the height of the dispute over Kaletra in 2005. As director of the Institute of Virology at the University of Maryland, Dr Gallo had been invited to speak at a conference sponsored by the Ministry of Health. In a number of press interviews during his stay, he stressed that he was a scientist with no status or expertise in the field of commerce. But he kept being asked and kept commenting more and more bluntly on the Kaletra dispute.

In one of his final interviews he warned two Brazilian journalists that their country needed to take care lest under pressure to reduce prices American drugs companies simply pulled out of Brazil. 'The drugs companies are not forced to work with Aids, okay? If I were the director of a company working with Aids and have problems with activists and the firm is not making money ... I would say: tell them to go to hell.'

On Brazilian pressure to get Abbott to reduce the price of Kaletra still further, Dr Gallo said: 'I know that Abbott would leave. Because they told me so. I received a telephone call before you got here. They say they will simply go away. That's that. They will bring the prices down to such and such and then they will go away. And then what will happen?'

Dr Gallo emphasized how individual American shareholders had invested their life savings in Abbott and now the activists wanted the company to give their drugs away. One of the journalists, Roseli Tardelli, who is herself an Aids activist, interjected.

'But poor people ...'

'Poor people, my ass,' replied Dr Gallo. 'We pay for poor people. You have money here, rich people. We have poor people in our country too. How can you talk about poor people to me?'

The struggle over prices and patents is set to continue. Beyond its domestic Aids responsibilities, Brazil has ambitions to promote its achievements abroad. It plans to provide free (unpatented) antiretrovirals to a number of small, Portuguese-speaking countries in Africa as well as to some of its Latin American neighbours. Big Pharma views such moves with distrust, seeing them as evidence that its global predominance is threatened by production and export from developing countries like Brazil, India and Thailand.

The United States and Brazil are at odds over almost every aspect of the fight against Aids. Brazil's successes have certainly not been achieved on the approved American pattern, so there is little chance that the lessons learned will get the international attention they deserve. The United States wants the world to adopt the Ugandan model with its emphasis on sexual abstinence. The Aids publications of Brazil's Ministry of Health continue to give overwhelming prominence to condoms, and almost none to abstinence.

In the sensitive area of condoms in schools, expressly forbidden in all American-funded programmes, the 2005 report of the Brazilian Aids programme stated that condoms were 'made available' to pupils aged 13 and above where the local community had been consulted. In pointing to the potential of this approach, it claimed that in two Brasilia secondary schools with strong sex education and Aids prevention programmes the number of teenage pregnancies had fallen from eighty a year to eight.

The report quoted a teacher as saying that it was better for condoms to be available inside rather than outside school. A pupil called Raul added: 'Quite often young people do not have enough money to buy condoms or are reluctant to ask for a condom from the health clinic.'

In rejecting American demands that it sign up to the anti-prostitution pledge, Brazil became the first country to turn down US funds to fight Aids. The US conditions caused upset and confusion elsewhere. USAID does not insist that UN agencies have formally to denounce prostitution, but almost everyone else has had to sign up – or lose American money.

At least two American organizations with an international role soon fell foul of the new proscription. Both took the US government to court. The first was DKT, the condom social marketing organization run by the sex industry entrepreneur Philip Harvey. DKT lost a $60,000 USAID contract for a further project in Vietnam because it would not sign the anti-prostitution pledge, and stood to lose further contracts worth millions. The second was the Open Society Institute, founded by the billionaire financier George Soros as a vehicle for his philanthropic work. At issue for the Soros agency was a regional Aids project run for USAID in Central Asia.

In challenging the government's 'unconstitutional and dangerous policy' in the US federal courts, the Open Society Institute complained that a refusal to sign the pledge meant that 'health workers across the world striving to stop HIV/Aids could lose funding and be forced to abandon life-saving programmes'.

In May 2006, as this edition of the book was going to press, both the Open Society Institute and DKT won their cases in federal courts in New York and Washington. The judges ruled that the anti-prostitution pledge was unconstitutional because it infringed freedom of speech. In the Washington case in which DKT was victorious, the judge declared that the Supreme Court 'has repeatedly held that the government may not compel private individuals or organizations to speak in a content-specific, viewpoint specific manner as a condition of participating in a government programme.' In plain language, it was unacceptable for the US government to try and force American citizens to think as it did as a condition for receiving federal funds. While government attorneys pondered their next move, Philip Harvey told his DKT staff in Vietnam to take up the reins of condom projects with USAID officials where they had been dropped a year ago when he refused to sign the pledge. Lives could now be saved among Vietnamese prostitutes and homosexuals as the result of a judicial intervention in distant Washington.

Other American organisations in the Aids field seeking federal dollars for their work, even those which had signed the pledge, were likely to be queuing at the desks of USAID officials to re-cast the terms of their projects. The impact of the judgement on foreign agencies looking for US money to fight Aids – including my old organization, the BBC World Service Trust, which in late 2005 had lost a USAID-funded project in Tanzania because it refused to sign the anti-prostitution pledge – would be minimal. The American right to freedom of speech, enshrined in the First Amendment, does not extend to foreigners.

In his first term in office, George W. Bush committed $350 million to action against sex trafficking. Backed by American power and prestige, this was an important initiative against one of the worst crimes of globalization. The American interest encouraged a number of governments, notably in the transition countries of the former Soviet Union, to attend to the sex trafficking scourge or face public admonishment from Washington. The problem lay in US determination to draw no distinction between the evils of sex trafficking and the pervasive reality of prostitution. George W. Bush and his supporters seriously contended that 'can-do' America could bring off significant and concrete results in both these areas before 2008, all for about $80 million a year.

Can prostitutes be rescued from their work? Can George W. Bush have an impact on the employment prospects of that ancient profession? At the Heritage Foundation, conservative inspiration for much of the Bush agenda, Jennifer Marshall, director of domestic policy, told me it was 'a wonderful idea that groups involved in the fight against Aids should be involved in helping to stop trafficking and free women from prostitution'.

Jennifer Marshall likened the abolitionist position on prostitution to that of slavery in the nineteenth century. 'If we put ourselves back 150 years and say "Look, we'll never get rid of slavery, we should just try and improve their conditions as slaves," it's absurd to think that now. But it was a plausible argument at the time. The utopian dream was to get rid of slavery. I would like to think we could make a serious dent in prostitution.

'The Bush administration is not going to eradicate prostitution, but it's going to take a swing at it, and with this amount of money [in the Aids programme] they're encouraging many others to take a swing at it as well. It's a five-year programme. Let's try it out.'

In 'trying it out', the Bush Aids programme was in danger of further compromising its Aids prevention efforts, already burdened by the emphasis on abstinence at the expense of condoms. From a domestic American perspective, there may be political attractions in working towards worldwide moral regeneration. But Aids is an immediate emergency and demands proven public health interventions. In Brazil as elsewhere, the recognition of prostitutes' rights has demonstrably saved lives. Denying funds to organizations not prepared to condemn prostitution puts lives at risk.

10

Crusaids against Drugs

'I don't deny the harm done by drugs, but my view is that the War on Drugs actually does even more harm than the drugs.'

George Soros

Within a week of George Bush's re-election in November 2004, Robert Charles, Assistant Secretary at the State Department in Washington, paid a visit to Antonio Maria Costa, head of the United Nations Office on Drugs and Crime in Vienna. This was the start of the 'Dear Bobby' episode which exposed something of the relationship between the superpower and a small UN agency.

Mr Charles avoided putting it this crudely, but those at the meeting took away a very clear impression of the message he conveyed: 'Okay, we are not going to give you more funds unless you stop supporting needle exchange.'

The United States is the largest donor to the UNODC, accounting for about a quarter of all its funding. In 2003 it gave $24 million. The next biggest contributor is Italy which always nominates the agency's executive director, another illustration of the way the money works.

In 2004 the significance of these arrangements went beyond influence and patronage. They had a direct bearing on the lives of hundreds of thousands of people at risk of getting sick and dying from HIV/Aids. The United States government was already out of step with most other countries in the world on how to respond to HIV infections from intravenous drug use. The United Nations was also supposed to be showing leadership, not ambivalence, in guiding the world's counter-attack on the epidemic.

According to the UN's own figures, half a million people are infected each year through shared and contaminated needles. That represents 10 per cent of the world's new infections. If you remove Africa from the equation, a third of all new HIV infections are the result of drug abuse. It has had a particularly severe impact on the former Soviet Union (nine out of ten HIV cases in Russia in 2002 were among intravenous drug users) and in South-east Asia. Dirty needles are a devastatingly effective way of spreading HIV and often account for the first stage in a chain reaction of infection. Because these drug-induced epidemics were growing fast, urgent and coherent action was required to slow their progress.

'Dear Mr Charles,' began the letter written by Mr Costa to the US Assistant Secretary on 11 November 2004, the day after their meeting. Mr Costa then scored out 'Dear Mr Charles' and inserted the friendlier, perhaps more ingratiating, 'Dear Bobby' by hand. 'I am glad that we were able to meet yesterday and had the chance to discuss a number of important matters.' There followed a review of what had been said about illicit drug production, notably in Afghanistan three years after the removal of the Taliban. It was on page two that Mr Costa proceeded to give Mr Charles a series of reassurances about needle exchange programmes which most of the world favoured and the United States did not. These are the programmes where addicts can swap used needles for clean ones so as to avoid the transmission of blood-borne diseases such as HIV. These programmes are generally grouped together as 'harm reduction', a term that Mr Costa used only in inverted commas.

'On the general issue of "harm reduction", I share your concern,' wrote Mr Costa. 'Under the guise of "harm reduction", there are people working disingenuously to alter the world's opposition to drugs. These people can misuse our well-intentioned statements for their own agenda, and this we cannot allow. Accordingly, and as we discussed in our meeting, we are reviewing all our statements, both printed and electronic, and will be more vigilant in the future.'

Mr Costa then directly addressed American opposition to needle exchange – 'or even needle giveaways, as you mentioned'. He said that the links between drug abuse and the Aids pandemic fuelled 'a well-known controversy'. That put UNODC in a difficult position, but he offered this concession: 'we neither endorse needle exchange as a solution for drug abuse, nor support public statements advocating such practices'.

Within days of the 'Dear Bobby' meeting, UNODC staff around the world received instructions from Vienna that they must avoid 'references to harm reduction and needle/syringe exchange' in official communications. They were also told to remove such terms from internal technical data. Why? Because computerized word searches have been used by conservative advocates in the US to identify and expose unAmerican approaches to problems that in their view require simple abstinence.

At the back of Mr Costa's mind in orchestrating these changes, perhaps, was the knowledge that the US had already removed funding from one UN organization. The United Nations Population Fund (UNFPA) works in the field of reproductive health and is a key player in UN programmes against Aids. It runs the UN's condom programme and takes responsibility for young people and Aids. Since the 1980s the Christian right in the US has accused UNFPA of being associated with China's coercive abortion policies, and the Republicans have consistently withheld funding. Under George W. Bush, there were a series of official US and international inquiries into UNFPA's role in China which declared this guilt by association to be wholly misplaced. But UNFPA has still been denied US government funds.

The United Nations Office on Drugs and Crime is one of ten UN organizations – UNFPA is another – that came together in the mid-1990s to establish UNAIDS. By bureaucratic mischance, UNODC was in the chair at UNAIDS when the needle exchange question reached crisis point in 2005. UNODC had been given specific responsibility to spearhead UN efforts to combat Aids in the area of intravenous drug use. Its lack of support for needle exchange and its open distrust of those who promoted it could hardly have come at a worse time.

There were two important dates in the 2005 diary for those who followed the UN conference trail on drug abuse and needle exchange. One was in Vienna in March and the other in Geneva in June. Both were a test of United Nations leadership in the Aids field. It would be no good demanding political resolve on the part of national governments if the responsible international bodies showed little of it.

The issue in Vienna was the level of backing that the Americans would receive in their objections to needle exchange. During a special debate on the subject, thirty countries rose to speak either in favour of the practice or in broader support of 'reducing the negative consequences of drug use'. Only two, Japan and South Korea, supported the American position. When Dr Peter

Piot, the Belgian head of UNAIDS, summed up the debate, he said there was 'clearly no consensus on harm reduction and needle exchange', an observation for which he was roundly criticized. There may well have been no unanimity on needle exchange, but Dr Piot's critics argued that he had missed an opportunity to stress how overwhelming was the international backing for 'harm reduction'.

Dr Piot, who has headed UNAIDS from the beginning, has an expertise and a concern that go back to his work on the early phases of the epidemic in Africa. He is also a considerable diplomat, as he has had to be to sustain any sort of forward momentum on Aids prevention in the era of George W. Bush and the Christian right. The test that many felt UNAIDS had fluffed in Vienna was restaged in Geneva three months later.

At issue there was an Aids prevention document which had been through draft after draft and which now came before the UNAIDS Programme Co-ordinating Board. Washington had already declared that it wanted the references to needle exchange removed. Among the weaknesses it detected in an early version of the document, the US Department of Health and Human Services singled out the need for more emphasis on leadership 'at all levels within governments but specifically at the top level' and then added without apparent irony: 'The US government does not support needle exchange programmes.'

Five words in the final UNAIDS document – 'sterile needle and syringe programmes' – could have scuppered agreement. Countries that favoured this well-tried approach were not going to give ground. The British, for instance, who had so far been very discreet in voicing their differences with the Americans on the Aids issue, decided that on this occasion they would publicly distance themselves from their allies. Gareth Thomas, a minister from the Department for International Development, went to Geneva to tell the UNAIDS board that the United Kingdom had 'a different approach' from the US. 'We support effective harm reduction programmes,' Mr Thomas said, 'especially needle and syringe exchange and methadone substitution therapy because they have been proved to reduce HIV infection among injecting drug users and their sexual partners in many countries.'

Rather than risk public isolation, the Americans backed off. Their opposition to needle exchange was noted, but they did not force a vote. The prevention document that emerged from the meeting was more mealy-mouthed on matters of sex and drugs than the robust calls for action of an earlier era, but at least the UN had upheld the international consensus on needle exchange.

For its part, the US was prepared to support programmes that treated addicts with the synthetic opiate methadone to wean them from heroin, but it was barred by Congress from funding clean needle projects. Officials running the Bush Aids programme faced their own policy challenge when the President announced in 2004 that he was adding a fifteenth country to those benefiting from his $15 billion Aids package. Vietnam became the only country in Asia to be included in the programme, and unlike the other fourteen, it was confronting an Aids epidemic demonstrably driven by intravenous drug use.

On his first visit to Vietnam as head of the US Aids programme in June 2004, Ambassador Randall Tobias commented that for the moment Vietnam's epidemic was confined largely to prostitutes and drug users but that it was 'on the verge of exploding into the general population'. The question he faced was whether congressional restrictions on buying clean needles or working with organizations committed to prostitutes' rights would undermine the effectiveness of US anti-Aids efforts.

Six out of ten Vietnamese with HIV have been infected through drug injection, and there is an immediate and frightening connection between drug abuse and prostitution. In the capital Hanoi one prostitute in six has been found to be a drug injector and in the port of Haiphong two in every five have reported that they inject. As the most efficient means of transmitting HIV, a contaminated needle can start a chain reaction of infection that begins, for example, with a male addict, proceeds to his sexual partners, often prostitutes, then to their clients and then through them to a wider population. Epidemiologists in Asia have created terrifying graphs showing how a single HIV-positive drug addict can be responsible for tens of thousands of infections.

A 2005 report on drugs and Aids in Asia produced by the 'Monitoring the Aids Pandemic Network' referred to political reluctance to provide clean injecting equipment 'fuelled in part by the notion that people who have never injected before will start injecting simply because clean needles are available'. It countered that 'in a review of over 400 surveillance reports and scientific papers undertaken for this report, no evidence was found that HIV prevention services for drug injectors, including the provision of clean needles, is associated with an increase in the number of people injecting drugs'.

As head of the Bush Aids programme, Ambassador Tobias took a judicious, even inscrutable, view of the controversy over clean needles. In an interview in September 2005 he told me that he had arrived in his new job 'with a totally clean sheet of paper' on this issue and had tried to appreciate both sides of the argument. 'On needle exchange people make a case that it's better to have somebody using clean needles than not,' he said. 'Other people make a case that if you're engaged in needle exchange then you're delaying getting that person off drugs.' He said that the

US policy was one of methadone substitution and that the ban on needle exchange did not stop the US from helping intravenous drug users in other ways. 'I confess to not having great technical expertise on this issue, but the policy makes sense to me.'

The US federal ban on needle exchange was introduced in the late 1980s as a Republican amendment to a Health and Human Services Bill and has been maintained throughout the Aids epidemic. As we have seen, President Clinton came close to lifting it when the US medical establishment unanimously declared that this would help fight Aids and not lead to more drug addiction. But he decided to stick with the politically less risky option of an all-out 'War on Drugs'.

In the Bush era of increased funding for Aids, the ban on funding needle exchange projects has resulted in the likely undermining of effective prevention efforts. At home in the United States, the picture is equally striking. Here the research data has also unequivocally demonstrated the value of needle exchange projects, yet the country must rely instead on a patchwork of state, city and local initiatives because of Washington's opposition to a more commonsensical approach.

Dr Don Des Jarlais is one of the world's leading epidemiologists in the drugs field. He was working in this area in New York before Aids struck, and when it did, he began studying cases among drug users before Aids had even been formally identified. He was an adviser to the British and the Dutch governments in the early years of their epidemics and conducted studies for the World Health Organization in cities which had needle exchange programmes and relatively low levels of HIV. I met Dr Des Jarlais at the Baron Edmond de Rothschild Chemical Dependency Unit in New York, where he is director of research. As an academic, he is not so much passionate about the merits of needle exchange as convinced that there is simply no room for legitimate doubt over the role it plays in limiting HIV infections.

The first Aids cases in New York were among gay men, said Dr Des Jarlais. The second group was gay men who also injected drugs. New York was the epicentre of the global spread of Aids. When Aids tests became available in the mid-1980s, the extent of the disaster became clear. Des Jarlais and his colleagues recorded a 50 per cent HIV infection rate among New York's drug injectors. He then travelled to Europe and Australia as these countries began to respond to their own Aids threat. 'New York was the big negative example that people didn't want replicated,' he said.

New York's response to Aids was bedevilled by politics from the start. First there was a disinclination to deal with a public health crisis among homosexuals. Then the public health priority was trumped by sensitivities over drugs. New York City had started a pilot needle exchange project in 1988, but the following year the city elected David Dinkins as its first black mayor and he closed it down. This was the time of the crack cocaine epidemic and increased violence linked to illegal drugs. There was also fierce opposition to needle exchanges among African Americans who resented being singled out as the target of drugs initiatives.

Needle exchange projects started again in New York in the early 1990s, but as underground initiatives and acts of civil disobedience. Only after they were up and running did the projects apply for legal waivers and start to function in the open. Then they received money from the city and the state, but there were still no federal government funds for their needle programmes.

I visited two needle exchange centres in New York City in May 2005. I had somehow imagined bright lights and shiny tiles, perhaps even medics in white coats dispensing medical paraphernalia in harsh and sterile conditions. I could not have got it more wrong. The Lower East Side Harm Reduction Centre and CitiWide Harm Reduction in the Bronx were relaxed and informal, striving with real signs of success to provide places of calm for people living desperately disordered lives.

The Lower East Side centre is sandwiched between food wholesalers for the Chinese restaurant trade. There was a commotion when I arrived as a dazed young woman who had overdosed that day and made it to the centre for help was coaxed into an ambulance and driven away. Then calm descended. I met Dr David Rosenthal, executive director of the centre, in a room set aside for Japanese Reiki therapy. Someone was playing a guitar in a nearby room. That all seemed to characterize the gentleness of the place and its approach. Certainly David Rosenthal was a very gentle exponent of the merits of treating drug addiction as something more than a crime.

The exclusive purpose of this harm reduction centre is to prevent Aids. It is not a treatment programme and it is not directed at getting people off drugs. Opponents argue that it should be about this larger objective, but would addicts then turn up and would infections be prevented? 'The problem with the treatment programmes', said Dr Rosenthal, 'is that they ask people, "Are you ready to stop?" If the answer's no, then it's goodbye.'

Regulars at the centre who decide they want to come off drugs are of course referred for treatment. 'If I had my way, I would like this to be a safe entry point for treatment,' said Dr Rosenthal, but it is still not the purpose of the centre. That is to provide a place for people on the very fringes of New York society so that they can begin to care about their own health and that of others. 'They begin to feel that they may be worth something.'

At the CitiWide project in the Bronx, I met Nancy Estrada, a former drug injector and now an assistant on the exchange programme. Around her were syringe kits, alcohol pads and little bottles of clean water, all of it given out in brown paper bags to the drug injectors who drop in. There were flyers with expressive diagrams and titles like 'Taking Care of Your Veins'. Four new people had enrolled on the programme that day, and twenty-nine in the previous month when 6,100 syringes were handed out and 4,800 returned.

Nancy described the progress that some addicts can make with the help of a project like CitiWide. 'People come for help first,' she said, 'then they come in for their syringes and now they want to go to detox.' That is what happened to her. 'You just don't want to do it any more. I love myself now, and I love CitiWide because they helped me.'

There is no question that these projects have worked. In 1992, when legal waivers allowed needle exchange projects to operate openly, 50 per cent of New York drug injectors were testing HIV-positive. In 2005 the figure dropped to 12 per cent. There was also a rapid fall in new infections among injecting drug users from 4 per cent a year in the early 1990s to less than 1 per cent.

The challenge to this hopeful picture comes from those determined to maintain and, if possible, extend the ban on needle exchanges. The argument against needles is the same as that used against condoms – that since HIV infections have continued to rise around the world, then the strategies used must be at fault and need to be overturned. In fact the precise reverse is more likely to be the case, certainly in the case of needle exchanges – that the reason these strategies have not always succeeded is that they have not been tried hard enough.

'I have not been seriously scientifically challenged,' Dr Des Jarlais told me. 'There are certainly a few syringe exchange programmes that didn't work – one in Vancouver; in Montreal; in Kathmandu. They were never implemented on the scale required to respond to the problem.' He said that the Vancouver and Montreal cases were complicated by cocaine epidemics that led to a huge increase in unsafe injections and a rapid increase in HIV infections. 'They then expanded the syringe exchange programmes and the transmission of HIV has gone down,' he said. 'Syringe exchange didn't control the epidemic mostly because the programmes weren't big enough.

'There are three cases out of about 500 where needle exchanges didn't work. This is taking the unusual situations, the outlier cases, and pretending that they are representative – and they're not.'

For New York's CitiWide Harm Reduction programme, federal opposition to needle exchange has led to a corresponding lack of support from some other official agencies. 'We are working in the area of public safety and public health,' said Daliah Heller, CitiWide's Canadian executive director. 'If there was a different federal attitude towards the war on drugs, we would have a better dialogue with the law enforcers. The War on Drugs people may believe that this will be eradicated, but we recognize that it won't go away. We're not drug legalizers. This is a health issue.'

The link between Aids and intravenous drug use introduced another important New York voice to the debate over criminalization and harm reduction. When George Soros spoke up, he did so with an independence of thought and means frankly denied even to the United Nations. Born in Hungary, he went on the run from the Nazis as a Budapest teenager, came to London after the Second World War and in due course made a fabulous fortune as a hedge-fund speculator in New York. He was the man who broke the pound in 1992 when sterling was forced out of the European

Exchange Rate Mechanism. Since that period, Mr Soros has spent much of that fortune in the former Soviet Union on democracy-building initiatives, then on human rights projects in the region and more recently back in the United States.

In Mr Soros's view, the War on Drugs is a doomed initiative. 'I don't deny the harm done by drugs, but my view is that the war on drugs actually does even more harm than the drugs,' he told me. 'By criminalizing the problem and treating it as a crime, you actually foster crime. It's a self-reinforcing process.'

It was the human rights aspect of drugs criminalization that first drew George Soros' Open Society Institute into a broader concern for the drug abusers themselves. In impoverished former Soviet bloc countries, the drugs explosion and the severity of the official response have led to more and more people, both users and petty dealers, spending longer and longer in jail. 'When Aids became a serious problem, we paid serious attention to it,' said Mr Soros. 'We pioneered harm reduction needle exchanges. We put troops on the ground, and then we got support from DFID [the British government's Department for International Development] and the US government – USAID. They also support our harm reduction programmes in Central Asia which are a model of how to deal with these things.'

Because of the US ban on using government money to buy clean needles, there had to be a mechanism for making sure they could still be supplied in quantity on USAID projects. The arrangement was that the agency paid for every aspect of these harm reduction programmes (clinics, administration, the heroin substitute methadone), but not the needles. Mr Soros had more than enough money to manage that.

In the course of 2005 this neat division of responsibility between the US government and the Soros organization began to fall apart. The problem was not the supply of clean needles to the projects in Central Asia – US officials held to the line that no federal American money was being spent on them – but the stipulation that all recipients of US Aids funds had to declare that they were opposed to prostitution. Mr Soros decided that the Open Society Institute would refuse to sign the pledge and take the US government to court. Towards the end of 2005 the likelihood was that the Institute's Central Asian harm reduction project would close prematurely, and that another small battle in the war against Aids would be lost.

George Soros's opposition to US drugs policy led to some bruising exchanges with leading Republicans in the 2004 presidential race in which he provocatively spent $27 million campaigning against George Bush's re-election. A former Speaker of the House of Representatives, Newt Gingrich, declared that Soros wanted Bush defeated 'because Soros wants to legalize heroin', while the present Speaker, Dennis Hastert, said in a TV interview in August 2004: 'I don't know where George Soros gets his money ... if it comes from overseas or from drug groups or where it comes from ... George Soros has been for legalizing drugs in this country. So, I mean he's got a lot of ancillary interests out there.'

Mr Soros told me that he saw such attacks 'as a validation of my position' and 'a demonstration of an extremist attitude which is part of the problem'. Not only were these allegations entirely bogus, but he also had no personal interest in taking this public stance on drugs policy. 'I have no drug problem myself. There is no drug problem in my family. It was purely an abstract, philosophical consideration.'

He said he likes to avoid the word 'legalization'. 'I talk about decriminalization. I am trying to break the black-and-white view where you're either a legalizer or a drugs warrior.' He told me that marijuana should 'probably' be legalized for everyone except children, that dealing in hard drugs should remain illegal, but that personal drug use should be decriminalized. 'You need to take measures to keep the harm done by drugs to a minimum and that includes the harm done in fighting drugs as well as the harm done by the drugs. "Harm Reduction" is the motto – for individuals and for communities. And you have to treat drug addiction as an addiction and not as a crime.'

Distinctions like these have failed to influence the public debate on drugs, even in the era of Aids. The very term 'harm reduction' is deeply suspect in the eyes of US officials, as the International Harm Reduction Association found to its cost. This small organization, with its headquarters in Australia and its executive director in London, was established to promote the success of British, Dutch and Australian needle exchange initiatives at the start of the Aids crisis in the 1980s. 'What we did in Britain was very, very significant,' said Professor Gerry Stimson, executive director of the association and a public health sociologist from Imperial College, London. 'Preventing HIV among drug injectors has been a public health success, but it's like other British inventions, we don't shout about it much.'

For a decade or more, the association made steady progress in urging international adoption of the 'harm reduction' formula that had succeeded in Europe and Australia. It also worked closely with the United Nations Office on Drugs and Crime, but that was before the US began its diplomatic arm-twisting. The association was then denied the UNODC funding which had been promised for international initiatives on 'harm reduction' and for bringing developing world law officers to its conferences. 'We're going backwards now because of the moralization of American foreign policy,' Professor Stimson told me.

Just how dirty the words 'harm' and 'reduction' were to the US administration became clear in a memo sent in February 2005 by a senior USAID official in Washington to every USAID office in Asia. The memo, subsequently leaked, was written in response to a congressional sub-committee's investigation into what was called 'the international harm reduction/drug legalisation movement'. USAID in Washington needed to report back quickly on the nature and extent of US engagement in harm reduction activities. Even conferences were suspect. 'Did any of your mission staff attend the International Conference on Harm Reduction in Chiang Mai (2003) or Melbourne (2004)?' the memo asked. 'Any plans to attend the 2005 meeting in Belfast? Did your mission provide support for any contractors or host country staff to attend these meetings?'

Like other experts on needle exchange whom I consulted for this book, Professor Stimson of the International Harm Reduction Association did not strike me as someone who is using Aids to subvert the world's opposition to illegal drugs. Yet this was what Mr Costa at UNODC, under pressure from the United States, accused many of these thoughtful and committed people of trying to do. It seemed to me, on the contrary, that the charge of disingenuousness could more readily be levelled at those who refuse to consider any qualification to a blanket crackdown on drugs. The moral righteousness behind appeals for abstinence accounted for the introduction of the US domestic ban on needle exchange. That has now been extended to Aids campaigning abroad where other institutions, notably the UN, have shown too little resistance. The cost, so far unquantifiable, is in new HIV infections and in lives.

11

Where Charity Begins

'How big does it have to get before you pay attention?'

'Don't Die of Ignorance' campaign, 1987

She is known in the courts by the initial 'N'. When her case reached its final stage in the House of Lords in May 2005, she was 30 years old and had been living in Britain for seven years. N is from the anarchic north of Uganda where at the age of 21 she was kidnapped by the terrorists of the Lord's Resistance Army. After being held captive for two years, she fell into the hands of Uganda's security forces by whom she was severely ill-treated and repeatedly raped. She escaped their clutches in 1998, arrived in London on false papers and applied for political asylum.

N was very ill when she reached Britain and within days she was admitted to Guy's Hospital where she was diagnosed with Aids. Until then she had not known why she was sick. She came to Britain to flee her terrible experiences in Uganda. There is no evidence she was motivated by the need for medical treatment. Thanks to the latest antiretroviral drugs, British doctors were able to save her life. Her fate was then at the mercy of British judges.

N applied for asylum on two grounds: first, that as a refugee she would be persecuted if she returned to Uganda; and second, under the European Convention on Human Rights, that to be returned to poor medical treatment, specifically a lack of the antiretrovirals that were keeping her alive, would be 'inhuman': she would probably die within a year or two. The Home Office initially refused her application, but she appealed to an adjudicator who found in her favour on the human rights claim. The Home Office next appealed to a higher immigration tribunal, but they too found in N's favour. The Home Office had by now lost two out of three rounds but pressed on for the result it wanted.

By a majority of two to one, the Court of Appeal in October 2003 found for the Home Office. That left N with only one chance in the British courts, an appeal to the House of Lords. Five law lords deliberated on her case and judgment was finally handed down on 5 May 2005. The Lords chose Election Day on which to release their thirty-page judgment. The press paid no attention whatsoever. Bad news for N had been comprehensively buried.

All five law lords expressed personal sympathy for N. Lord Nicholls of Birkenhead said that her return to Uganda would be 'similar to having a life-support machine switched off'. He said that no one could fail to be touched by N's plight and that the case had left him with a 'lasting sense of deep sadness'. Lord Walker of Gestingthorpe agreed that the humanitarian case was 'very powerful indeed. None of us wishes to send a young woman, who has already suffered so much but is now well cared for and with a future ahead of her, home to the likelihood of an early death in a much less favourable environment.'

But one after another, by a majority of five to nil, the law lords crushed N's appeal to stay in Britain. 'This is a very sad case but it is, unfortunately, not exceptional,' said Lord Walker. The unanimous judgment appeared to turn on the fact that N was not actually dying at present and that the question was whether her prospects back in Uganda were so dire that acute suffering or early death could be attributed directly to her removal. 'Is that test satisfied here?' asked Lord Brown of Eaton-under-Heywood. 'Much though I would prefer not to have to make this decision, I for my part feel driven to answer no to this question.'

The fate of several hundred other HIV-positive asylum-seekers also facing deportation hung on the outcome of N's case. She herself was not immediately deported, and it was likely that her case would be taken to the European Court of Human Rights for further and final judgment. At the end of his legal opinion Lord Brown said that the Home Secretary could himself show clemency and allow N to stay, but he underlined the costs of doing so. 'The choice now is between allowing the patient to remain in the host state to enjoy decades of healthy life at the expense of that state ... and deporting the patient to a life of rapidly declining health leading to a comparatively early death.' He defined the costs as continuing medical treatment and welfare benefits, but also 'in terms of immigration control' for those in similar circumstances in the queue.

'Immigration control' was the political guts of this matter. The political parties had just fought a long and corrosive election campaign in which Michael Howard's Conservatives had emphasized the perils of immigration and then, explosively, linked it with the global Aids epidemic.

At the outset of the campaign in January 2005 Mr Howard was reckoned to have seized the electoral initiative when he claimed that only the Conservatives had 'the courage to tell the truth about immigration'. A few weeks later he announced that a Conservative government would introduce compulsory health tests for migrants, specifically for HIV and tuberculosis which often infect the same patients. A significant element in Britain's growing sexual health crisis was an increase in HIV infections, and among those acquiring it heterosexually a high proportion had done so in Africa. The Conservatives put this figure at 80 per cent, and then in an election poster, described by one liberal commentator as 'toxic', declared: 'It's not racist to want to control immigration.'

For a while it seemed that Labour would compete on the same soiled turf as the Tories, but they ended up rejecting specific Conservative proposals for HIV tests. The truth was that Labour was unlikely to be outflanked by the Conservatives on matters of immigration and Aids. Earlier initiatives on 'health tourism' had seen to it that Labour was very much in tune with popular prejudices concerning both.

A year before the general election the government had tightened up the rules over how overseas visitors were to be charged for health services. In future anyone in the country without proper authority – illegal immigrants and people who had been refused asylum or whose visas had expired – would be billed for their National Health Service treatment. Until then any immigrant, regardless of legal status, had been entitled to free health care after twelve months in the country. On the face of it, the beefing up of the rules seemed a reasonable safeguard against those intent on exploiting the system. The measure, however, had a number of damaging effects. It was particularly harsh on people with HIV, it had serious implications for public health, and it flew in the face of Britain's zealously promoted role as a leader in the worldwide fight against Aids.

In order to protect the community at large, the treatment of some communicable diseases has always been free of charge. They include TB and a number of sexually transmitted infections, but they exclude HIV/Aids. The reason for this is partly historical and partly financial. When the lists were originally drawn up, there was no effective treatment for HIV/Aids. When treatment did become available, it was expensive, and the National Health Service did not want to take on the extra expense.

To compel illegal immigrants and failed asylum seekers to pay for their Aids treatment is the same as denying them that treatment. These are not 'health tourists' with bank balances. Most of them have no money at all. They are also unlikely even to be 'health tourists'. What little evidence there is suggests that medical treatment is not a motive for travel. The Department of Health admitted in 2005 that it had conducted no research of its own into 'health tourism' among HIV-positive migrants – adding to the impression that the objective was political before it was financial – but the Terrence Higgins Trust, the Aids charity that has impressively pursued this along with other key policy matters, had done some of the Department's work for it.

The Trust surveyed sixty HIV-positive migrants who had recently used its own services and those of the George House Trust in the north-west of England. Only two of the sixty had been diagnosed before they reached Britain and only 8 per cent were diagnosed within three months of arrival. Three-quarters of them waited for more than nine months before having an HIV test and fully a third did not have a test for more than eighteen months. These figures confirmed my own less scientific findings. Listening to African asylum seekers in London who were also HIV-positive, the stories that unfolded were of the ill treatment and hardship at home that led them to seek better lives in Britain rather than the desire to seek medical help.

The Terrence Higgins Trust came up with stark individual examples of the way the new charges were driving patients from treatment. It said it knew of at least two pregnant women effectively refused the treatment that would prevent the transmission of HIV to their unborn children. 'This is particularly cruel and short-sighted,' said the Trust, 'since such treatment is relatively inexpensive, highly efficacious, and prevents the child becoming a burden on the state in future years.' It further reported that a number of doctors were continuing their care for HIV-positive migrants despite the new government rules. But medical ethics and common humanity were no substitute for sensible rules.

The exclusion of HIV from the communicable diseases for which free treatment is available threw up situations which posed a wider risk. The Terrence Higgins Trust reported cases where HIV-positive people infected with TB were told that the TB treatment was free but that they would be charged for their HIV treatment. The result was that treatment for both was abandoned, with potentially serious consequences for all their contacts. People who had both HIV and other sexually transmitted infections such as gonorrhoea or chlamydia could be treated for the last two, but not the first. 'It is a strange logic which enables people to access free treatment for gonorrhoea on the grounds of public health,' the Trust commented, 'but not for the potentially fatal, and equally transmissible, HIV.'

There was also the matter of the bureaucratic revolving door. Everyone in Britain is entitled to emergency care, and this is invariably more expensive than ongoing treatment for a serious condition. Again, the Terrence Higgins Trust provided a telling illustration of how this worked in practice. One immigrant without residence papers went to a North London hospital suffering from pneumonia linked to her HIV-positive status. When she was billed £2,000 for four days of treatment, she couldn't pay and left. She later collapsed and was brought back to Accident and Emergency where she was treated at an estimated further cost of £23,000. The average cost of keeping someone healthy on antiretroviral treatment is less than £10,000 a year.

In addition to caring and campaigning organizations like the Terrence Higgins Trust, other voices were raised over the effects of the decision to charge poor migrants for their HIV treatment. A panel of four leading Aids specialists, led by Professor Brian Gazzard of the Chelsea and Westminster Hospital, produced a report in March 2005 declaring that the rule-tightening would make Britain's HIV epidemic worse. The decision might make 'sound political sense,' their report said, 'but for HIV the public health and economic costs will outweigh any benefits'.

The panel pointed to the steady rise in HIV infections in Britain – from 2,800 new cases in 1998 to 5,700 in 2002 and 6,600 in 2003 – and said that it was 'wholly irrational' to exclude HIV from the list of communicable and sexually transmitted infections for which treatment was always available. The four physicians wanted HIV reclassified as a disease warranting free medical treatment. They concluded: 'We believe the cost savings and deterrent effect of refusing treatment are negligible though the public health consequences are great.'

Then the House of Commons Health Committee weighed in. After hearings early in 2005, including a long and pointed session with the public health minister Melanie Johnson, the committee reported that they were 'not convinced that the government has fully understood the complexity and breadth of the issues involved in charging for HIV treatment, and the potential consequences of getting it wrong …

'Firstly, if free treatment is not available, people may be deterred from taking an HIV test, and will remain in the community undiagnosed and infectious. Secondly, research evidence suggests that HIV treatment can in fact lower an individual's infectivity significantly, reducing the potential for onward transmission.

'It is a nonsense that the government is prepared to fund a person's TB treatment on public health grounds but not treatment of his HIV infection. Untreated HIV-positive people living in this country present a serious public health threat, and we have therefore recommended that all HIV-positive people, regardless of their immigration status, receive free treatment to reduce the likelihood of the onward transmission of HIV, of mother-to-child transmission of HIV, and of the onward transmission of TB.' To achieve this, said the committee, simply required the reclassification of HIV as a sexually transmitted infection. Since HIV is indeed spread overwhelmingly through sex, this did not seem to set a damaging precedent.

In their detailed response to the committee's report in July 2005, ministers made one concession. They said they had never intended to charge pregnant women, whatever their immigration status, for HIV treatment to prevent mother-to-child transmission. They had accordingly reissued the guidance to clear up 'some uncertainty within the NHS on how to respond to such cases'. For the rest of the committee's recommendations, ministers stood firm against providing 'a free service for illegal immigrants or failed asylum seekers, or others with no legal right to be living here. The government does not accept that such persons with HIV should receive free treatment without question.' The National Health Service had always had powers to charge for these services, 'all we have done is to make it more difficult for people who should not be receiving them free of charge to take advantage of the system'.

Apart from potential public health consequences for Britain, there was another fault line in the government's refusal to respond to demands to reconsider the HIV treatment charges. It did not sit at all comfortably with British professions to be leading international efforts to bring comprehensive help to bear on Africa's Aids disaster. Britain's humanitarian commitment to Aids in Africa seemed strictly limited to Africans who stayed there.

The British push for international Aids leadership began in 2004. This was in the run-up to the 'Year of Africa' in 2005 when Tony Blair was to head both the G8 and the European Union and when the continent's troubles would top the international agenda. 'Ignoring the issue of Aids is simply not an option,' Tony Blair declared in July 2004 at the launch of a new British strategy for tackling the disease in the developing world. The strategy was underpinned by an announcement from Gordon Brown, Chancellor of the Exchequer, that Britain would spend £1.5 billion over three years on Aids in the poor world. Next to the United States, the United Kingdom was to be the world's largest national donor in the fight against Aids. 'Together the world can make a huge difference,' said Mr Blair, 'and I am determined that Britain will take the lead.'

The Department for International Development, the British aid ministry, has a reputation for being one of the best of the national agencies. Unlike its United States counterpart USAID, DFID is able to put development theory and development practice before the pressures of politics. It has also seen its budget increase dramatically in the years of Gordon Brown's chancellorship. DFID would be spending the new Aids money on a strategy that included big increases in treatment, and one of its essential justifications was the impact that more Aids treatment could have on the spread of the disease.

'There is now an international consensus that treatment and care are essential parts of an effective and comprehensive response to Aids,' stated another DFID policy document. 'As well as the direct benefits for people receiving it, access to treatment and care can help prevention efforts and programmes designed to minimize the impact of Aids. Availability of ART [antiretroviral therapy] in particular gives people a reason to seek testing, and it might reduce the level of transmission in a population.'

This was the precise case advanced by critics of the government's decision to tighten up on HIV treatment for illegal immigrants in Britain – that the availability of treatment itself encouraged people to come forward for testing and reduced the likely spread of the virus. It was an argument that ministers were happy to advance for the rest of the world but which they set aside for Britain. It was not a good example of Mr Blair's ambitions for 'joined-up government'.

At the climax to his 'Year of Africa' in July 2005, the Prime Minister gained the agreement of his fellow G8 leaders to set another target in the world's response to Aids. The World Health Organization had set the benchmark at 3 million HIV-positive people under treatment by the end of 2005. The United States had raised the bar by declaring that through the Bush programme they alone would insure that 2 million people were on drugs by the end of 2008. Now the final Gleneagles communiqué committed the rich world as a whole to coming 'as close as possible to universal access to treatment for all those who needed it by 2010'.

Even allowing for the equivocal 'as close as possible', this was an impressive objective. To realize it would require paying massive attention to rebuilding the health systems of Africa's poorest countries, for only then could treatment be effectively delivered.

Still, the rich world had at least made it consistently plain that there would be no political barrier to providing the drugs themselves. In the case of Britain, however, a formidable inconsistency remained. Here was a government seeking to lead the way in providing universal Aids treatment in the poor world, whatever the challenges, but resisting the same objective at home where provision was far more easily achieved. Treatment for poor Africans in Britain continued to depend on their immigration status.

The record of the Blair government on Aids to date is the mirror image of that of the Conservatives under Margaret Thatcher two decades earlier. Lady Thatcher's interest in Third World development was at best modest and intermittent. She viewed African poverty almost entirely through the need to counter the continent's socialist economics and the strategic threat posed by the Soviet Union. Yet under her prime ministership Britain developed one of the most effective domestic responses to Aids of any country in the world.

'I don't think Margaret had a great deal of natural sympathy in this area,' said Lord Fowler, who as Norman Fowler was Thatcher's longest serving Health and Social Security Secretary. 'At the beginning I think she suspected that the threat of Aids was rather overdone. She accepted that we had to do something in terms of warning people, but I don't think she felt we had to do anything particularly high-profile.'

Norman Fowler had been Health Secretary for more than four years when in November 1985 he authorized the first British Aids information campaign. Aids cases then numbered about 250, but the rate of increase was assuming American proportions. 'There was no vaccine and no cure,' he told me. 'All you could do was to warn people what the dangers were. If you didn't warn them, you were going to have unnecessary deaths.' Twenty years later, honest information campaigns remain the best vaccine.

Fowler is a former journalist and has a bluff, matter-of-fact approach to the world. By the end of 1985 he was also ready for a new challenge, although few public figures would choose Aids to make their mark. 'There is always an embarrassment factor,' he said. 'You are either liable to be pilloried or laughed at.'

Mrs Thatcher's response to drafts of the first press advertisements was not encouraging. Health Department officials received a message from Downing Street saying, 'She wants to know if they have to go into the newspapers.' Officials asked where else they were expected to go. 'She was wondering about lavatory walls – like that old information they used to have about VD.'

The way round the Thatcher problem was to make sure she had no direct say in decisions. A special cabinet sub-committee to deal with Aids was set up under the Deputy Prime Minister William Whitelaw. Lady Thatcher had once famously observed of her deputy, 'Every Prime Minister needs a Willie.' Lord Fowler told me that Whitelaw was 'a very different kettle of fish. He was very practical, very down-to-earth and had been in the army, as he said at our first meeting.'

From 1986 safe sex and condom promotion became the key campaign themes of the Thatcher government's response to Aids. Norman Fowler claimed that he was responsible for putting the word 'condom' back into English usage. It was as controversial an approach then as it became in the era of President George W. Bush. At a time when the Reagan administration was still steering clear of the subject, the Thatcher government was sending 23 million leaflets entitled 'Aids – Don't Die of Ignorance' through the nation's letter boxes.

The leaflet was certainly to the point. 'Because the virus can be present in semen and vaginal fluid, this means for most people the only real danger comes through having sexual intercourse with an infected person. This means vaginal or anal sex. (It could also be that oral sex can be risky particularly if semen is taken into the mouth.) So the virus can be passed from man to man, man to woman and woman to man.'

Television advertisements on the theme of 'Don't Die of Ignorance' ran from early 1987. The actor John Hurt provided the sonorous voice-over. 'How big does it have to get before you pay attention?' The advertisements featured tombstones and icebergs and did not have the explicitness of the leaflets. One commentator complained that they suggested that 'the disease could be caught from hewing granite or cruising the North Pole'.

Even so, it was Aids that brought the first condom advertisements on to British television. A decade earlier an effort to promote them as contraceptives had been rejected by the commercial television authorities on the grounds that it 'would be felt to be offensive by a large section of the public'. Condom advertisements are rarely screened by the major American networks, and they provoke outcry when they are.

In shaping the British response to Aids, Norman Fowler said he received all the help he needed from British television, but much less from religious leaders. The most that could be said of the churches and the other faiths was that they did not publicly stand in the way of the health campaign. While Christian leaders simply remained 'off the air', in Lord Fowler's phrase, the Chief Rabbi, Sir Immanuel Jakobovits, presented the minister with a memorandum that complimented him on the 'urgency, boldness and effectiveness' of the campaign but then provided a list of no fewer than fourteen reasons for objecting to it.

'It tells people not what is right, but how to do wrong and get away with it,' the Chief Rabbi complained. It was like 'instructing thieves how to escape being caught ... Say plainly, Aids is the consequence of marital infidelity, premarital adventures, sexual deviation and social irresponsibility – putting pleasure before duty and discipline.'

Fowler maintained his focus and stoutly rejected approaches that could diminish the impact of practical advice. His judgement has as much relevance after twenty-five years of Aids as it did in those early years. 'We never argued in favour of a "condom society," ' he wrote in his memoirs *Ministers Decide* in 1991. 'We used every opportunity to underline the value of one loving partner. But there is a limit to how effective government can be in changing the whole moral climate of society ... There is no intrinsic reason why government ministers cannot argue for chastity and sex only within marriage, but that would not have been remotely enough in 1986.'

Perhaps out of respect for her fiercer supporters, Mrs Thatcher continued to keep her distance from the awkward judgements posed by the Aids crisis. Yet whenever asked, she backed the pragmatic approach. According to Lord Fowler, her only direct intervention came when it was proposed that there should be a ministerial broadcast on the dangers of Aids. 'Norman,' she told her Health Secretary, 'I didn't even have a ministerial broadcast for the Falklands. I'm certainly not going to have one for this.'

The measured public health response to Aids in Britain had its impact on one of the most important constituencies of all, HIV-positive people themselves. Among the Aids organizations that helped me with this book is NAM, formerly the National Aids Manual, which had its origins in the early years of the epidemic among British gays and which now provides a wealth of information for HIV-positive people and HIV practitioners. When I visited their offices in South London, I met Michael Carter, one of NAM's regular contributors and the author of a book called *Living with HIV*.

Michael told me about his HIV diagnosis in 1991, his Aids-related pneumonia in 1994 and how he believed he would die. Since 1998 he has been on antiretrovirals and has his life back. 'I feel completely well most of the time,' he told me. 'I have ceased to regard myself as someone who is ill. I take it as granted that I am fit and healthy, probably fitter and healthier than my peer group.' To make the point, he has run three full marathons and dozens of half marathons since 2000.

With the balance and precision of the academic historian that he is, Michael told me a little of his experiences as a gay man who is also HIV-positive – the irksome prejudice of some health professionals and the 'low-grade harassment' he faced from local yobs when they learned that he had acquired his housing association flat on the Thames at Rotherhithe because he had HIV. 'The police could not have been more supportive,' he added.

When we discussed the early years of Aids in Britain, Michael said: 'When I go to international conferences or talk to other HIV organizations overseas, I'm always immensely proud of the British response to HIV. Health promotion was put before prejudice. Treatment was provided within the NHS and drugs are provided regardless of cost. If I compare the level of treatment I receive with the level of treatment my parents receive with chronic heart and lung conditions, I'm glad I've got HIV.'

There was one Aids challenge facing the Thatcher government that was more politically charged even than the promotion of safe sex. The conflict between the War on Drugs and the public priority of tackling the epidemic divided America at home and detracted from American Aids efforts worldwide. It also threatened for a time to set the United Nations against itself. In Britain, it separated England and Scotland, and set Scottish ministers against their United Kingdom counterparts.

Aids took off at a time when heroin in the Western world was becoming cheaper and more plentiful. This was the period of the Soviet invasion of Afghanistan and the fall of the Shah of Iran when that region took over from South-east Asia as the principal source for hard drugs. The question for the health authorities in the West was how to respond to the risk that intravenous drug users posed to themselves and others. Was criminalization and crackdown a sufficient public policy response? Scottish ministers believed it was. The English did not. So exasperated did London become with Edinburgh's prohibitionist fervour that a health minister south of the border exploded at one stage: 'Bugger the Scots!'

The problem for the Scots was that the link between drug abuse and Aids was at its strongest on their own doorstep. In the first years of the epidemic there were no tests for HIV, but the alarm bells had begun to ring. Dr Roy Robertson, a GP working in the Muirhouse estate on the outskirts of the city, was saying from the early 1980s that Edinburgh risked a serious epidemic. When tests became available in the middle of the decade, researchers tested the stored blood of 164 of Dr Robertson's drug-injecting patients and found that 83 of them tested positive for HIV – a rate of 50 per cent.

If the public interest lay in containing Aids rather than punishing addicts, the answer was needle exchange. This was Norman Fowler's approach from the beginning. 'Scottish ministers had an issue with that,' he told me. 'That never seemed to me to be entirely logical given that they had by far the biggest problem.'

Not only did Scottish ministers resist this logic. They presided over a criminal justice and a health system that went to great lengths to exclude drug users. When, for instance, HIV tests became available, heroin injectors who were shown to be clear of the virus were specifically denied access to methadone treatment. This meant that if an addict already had the virus, he would receive the substitution therapy. If he was at real risk of becoming infected, he would not. Official Scottish attitudes were diligently promoting the HIV epidemic.

Police warnings led to the closure in the early 1980s of the only pharmaceutical supplier in Edinburgh where addicts could buy clean needles. Even the possession of a needle could lead to prosecution. More commonly, I was told by one former addict, police would confiscate needles and syringes on the street and crush them under their boots. These tactics led directly to the city's infamous 'shooting galleries' where, to avoid arrest for possession, addicts and dealers would complete all their business behind closed doors, including of course the sharing of needles and the passing on of HIV.

The justice system in Scotland played its own part. A new sentencing policy invoked a 'showcase' response to drugs in which pushers were imprisoned for ten years or more. The Muirhouse GP Roy Robertson spent time in court as an expert witness and on behalf of his own patients. 'The understanding here was that heroin users were evil people and were committing a crime. People in possession of two grams of heroin were committing a serious crime and people who admitted to buying a bit of heroin and sharing it with their mates were drug dealers. They were being sentenced for ten years for supplying heroin. All they were was pathetically addicted to drugs. It was a punitive society.'

As the Edinburgh epidemic intensified, the policy-makers had to think again. Early in 1986 the Scottish Office announced that it was setting up a committee under Dr Brian McClelland, a senior blood transfusion official, to examine the whole issue of drug abuse. It would pronounce on the vital matter of needle exchange. But just a couple of weeks before the committee was due to report, the minister who set it up decided to make his own pronouncement on the subject. John Mackay, a former teacher from Oban, was described as having 'particularly strong views on moral issues'. His interview with *The Scotsman* in September 1986 was seen as an effort to anticipate and undermine any liberal-minded conclusions from the committee.

Mackay first made it plain that he resented spending money and effort 'on a disease which could easily be prevented by people changing their lifestyles'. At the same time he was optimistic that Aids would not assume the gravest proportions in Britain because 'the lifestyles that encourage the spread are not as prevalent in this country as they are in places like California'.

He accepted that supplying clean needles would slow down the spread of Aids but was convinced that it 'would bring more people into the heroin addiction world. The fact of the matter is the best thing they can do is to stop their heroin addiction.' What if the committee he had appointed recommended needle exchange? 'I am personally, and on principle, against it. It goes against my own view of these matters. I just think heroin addiction is wrong, that we ought not as a government, as a country, [to] be encouraging it by giving people the means.' There was a final hint of menace directed at doctors like Dr Robertson who favoured needle supply. That would be a real problem for the police, the Minister said, 'because certain doctors will be then aiding and abetting people in what is a criminal activity'.

The McClelland committee duly reported in favour of needle exchange. It concluded that clean needles should not be denied to addicts, and it bluntly spelled out the public health equation that 'the threat to life by the spread of HIV is greater than that of drug use'.

This was a crucial turning-point against a policy limited to crackdown and criminalization in Scotland, and the beginning of a decline in Aids in Edinburgh. There has been a marked fall in the number of heroin users becoming infected with HIV, peaking at more than 200 in 1986 and down to single figures since 1998. New Aids cases among intravenous drug users rose to almost 50 a year in the mid-1990s but had also fallen to single figures by the end of the century. Edinburgh still has its drug problem, but the political tug-of-war of the 1980s has radically changed things. 'If it hadn't been for HIV/Aids, we'd still be in the Stone Age as far as drug users are concerned,' said Dr Robertson. 'That was the only thing that got sensible treatment for drug-users off the mark.'

In August 2005 I visited 'The Exchange' in Spittal Street under the eaves of Edinburgh Castle. It is run by the local National Health trust and is located in a converted church. Like the projects I visited in New York, it combined purpose and commitment with informality. I met Michael McCullough there. He is a politics and philosophy graduate of Glasgow University and one-time Edinburgh bus driver who told me how he had become a heroin addict twenty-five years ago. 'I'd been on cannabis for ten years and that was doing me no harm,' he said. 'They had lied to me about that, so I thought they were lying to me about the dangers of heroin.'

When I met him, Michael McCullough had been on the heroin substitute methadone for six months and things were going well.

I asked him what he thought about ventures like the Spittal Street Centre. 'Without this place,' he replied, 'there would be at least another 1,500 on the streets. They'd have every chance of developing Hepatitis C and HIV, and no chance of getting off the heroin.'

In her book *Aids in the UK*, on the Conservative government's record in the 1980s and early 1990s, Virginia Berridge of the London School of Hygiene and Tropical Medicine challenged and demolished the idea that Margaret Thatcher had brought a 'New Right' perspective to bear on the epidemic. In fact the Thatcher experience 'underlined the exact opposite'. The policy consensus that emerged on tackling Aids in Britain 'stressed a liberal middle-of-the-road type of approach. This was advice for safe sex, not no sex; it was, eventually, harm minimisation for drug users, not prohibition of drug use. It was the consensual strategy of health education, from which no one could dissent.'

Dr Berridge was writing in 1995, six years before George W. Bush began laying the foundations for a truly 'New Right' approach to Aids in the United States and around the world. Not only was sexual abstinence stressed, but the immorality of prostitution had to be condemned and there could be no support for needle exchange. It will take until the end of the decade before the effectiveness of the rival approaches – public health consensus versus faith-based morality – can be assessed. But progress in combating Aids at home in the United Kingdom and in the United States might offer a pointer. According to UNAIDS statistics published in 2004, America has an adult HIV prevalence rate six times greater than that of Britain.

12

Condom Wars

'We said that the condom is a girl's best friend.'

Senator Mechai Viravaidya, Thailand

Historians have traced the origin of the condom to the ancient world, but its use as protection against sexually transmitted disease dates from the syphilis epidemic which reached Europe 500 years before Aids. There is even some condom research dating from the sixteenth century. The Italian anatomist Gabriello Fallopio wrote a treatise on *The French Disease* in which he advised men to use 'a small linen cloth made to fit the glans' and claimed that he had 'tried the experiment on 1,100 men, and I call immortal God to witness that not one of them was infected'.

Arguments over their reliability, how they blunt sexual pleasure and, above all, the moral and religious issues raised by sexual disease have surrounded condoms from the beginning. The oldest physical examples we have were dug up at Dudley Castle, in the West Midlands, where a latrine was sealed up after the castle fell to Parliamentary forces in the English Civil War. Archaeologists found that 'the deposit had composted nicely into a peaty mass' from which they extracted five used and five unused condoms. It is tempting to speculate that it was Royalist libertines inside the castle who were making use of them while disapproving Puritans conducted the siege.

Disapproval predominates in the historical record. An eighteenth-century German venereologist doubted whether the condom worked properly: 'This shameful invention suppresses and annihilates completely the only natural end of cohabitation, namely procreation ... finally, they are insufficient to assure immunity, for the least hole will permit contagion.' In the United States the 1873 Comstock Act broadened the definition of obscenity to include information on 'the prevention of conception', and the sending of condoms through the post became illegal for the next hundred years.

The need for birth control in the modern era led to widespread acceptance of the condom. Only prudishness and embarrassment limited its promotion. With the Aids disaster, fundamental arguments about sexual morality have again arisen. They have played out in every country in the world and have often limited effective national responses. Those societies that have dealt openly and pragmatically with the threat of sexual infection and that have been prepared to make condoms the central part of an anti-Aids strategy appear to have been the most successful in containing the epidemic.

In Thailand they call the condom a *mechai* after the man who did so much to make its use acceptable. Not everyone would want such a product named after him, but for Senator Mechai Viravaidya it is a badge of honour. He is quite unembarrassed about promoting condoms. He blows them up in front of tittering schoolteachers. He hands out chocolate-flavoured ones to his fellow senators – and smaller ones, lemon-flavoured, to members of the lower house. He wears them on his fingers for publicity photographs. He runs a successful Bangkok restaurant called 'Cabbages and Condoms' where the dinner bill comes not with a free mint but with a give-away condom. There is nothing, however absurd or outrageous, that Senator Viravaidya will not do to popularize condoms. There is also nothing remotely frivolous about him or his activities. His underlying purpose is stern and focused.

Mechai's long affair with the condom began in the 1960s. By then this son of a Thai father and a Scottish mother was already a professional economist, a TV soap star, a man about town and a budding politician. It was another of his careers, part-time journalism, that introduced him to the challenge Thailand faced from its population explosion. He agreed to take over family planning campaigns for the recently established Planned Parenthood Association of Thailand and later formed his own population and development organization. His shameless addiction to condom promotion was under way.

'If soldiers are embarrassed by guns, you will lose the war,' he says.

The family planning revolution in parts of Asia has been one of the few successes chalked up to development interventions in the past forty years. In Thailand, the birth rate and population growth halved between the 1960s and the 1980s. Instead of the population doubling every twenty-one years, as it threatened to do in the 1960s, it is now set to double every forty-four years, and the birth rate is still falling. In the 1960s, 3 per cent of couples were using contraception; in 1984, 65 per cent were doing so.

However embarrassing the condom and however awkward the discussions surrounding it, family planning campaigns could always be assumed to be about sex within faithful heterosexual marriages. No such assumptions could be made when Aids arrived in Thailand in the mid-1980s. The first patient was a Thai homosexual who had been living in America. When the epidemic took off towards the end of the decade, the *mechai*, both the man and the product, came into their own.

Initially, little public attention was paid to Aids in Thailand as the country geared up for the foreign tourist boom. One official notoriously remarked that there was no evidence of 'Thai-to-Thai' HIV transmission and a senior bureaucrat at the Ministry of Public Health gave the game away with this gobbledegook: 'The government is approaching the Aids problem step by step in accordance with the degree of the problem, suitability and timing, while in the implementation of each action attempting to cause as little impact on the country as a whole.'

The first epidemic wave was among intravenous drug users where prevalence rose in the single year 1988–9 from 0 per cent to 40 per cent. The next group were prostitutes, with more than two out of five in the northern resort of Chiang Mai testing HIV-positive in 1989. When a further study was conducted and the women were stratified by price, the cheapest charging from 75p to £1.25 recorded a ghastly HIV rate of 72 per cent, the next group charging between £1.25 and £2.50 had a rate of 30 per cent and the most expensive charging more than £2.50 recorded 16 per cent. It was a grim illustration of how the poor always bear the brunt of Aids.

Despite the government's foot-dragging in response to the crisis, there was another set of statistics that Mechai deployed to achieve his first big breakthrough. HIV was growing at an alarming rate among army recruits, reaching more than 500 in an intake of 26,000 in 1990. He persuaded army chiefs to give him access to the 320 radio stations and the two TV channels they controlled, and anti-Aids messages were heavily promoted for the next three years. Civilians continued to resist appeals for a robust response – Mechai accused the Prime Minister of being more interested in golf than Aids – but the perplexing machinations of Thai politics came to the rescue early in 1991 when the army staged a coup and replaced one civilian government with another more to its liking.

The new Prime Minister was Anand Panyarachun, an urbane former diplomat and head of the Thai foreign service. He appointed Mechai Viravaidya as a minister in the Prime Minister's office and offered him responsibility for tourism and the media. Mechai countered that he wanted responsibility for Aids as well, and then persuaded Anand to take a direct and personal interest in a vigorous national prevention effort. The Aids budget was increased twenty-fold in the course of the next two years, the media onslaught on Aids became intense and Thailand did it all without foreign aid. It was a textbook case of how to deal with the epidemic.

Thailand's tourist officials were appalled. Sex was a sly part of Thailand's appeal to foreigners, and now the minister in charge was saying you could sicken and die from sex in Thailand. Mechai was unrepentant. He had already expressed his distaste for sex tourism and then he went on TV to advise such tourists not to fly to Thailand: 'They should buy rat poison and stay at home and take it instead.'

The head of Thailand's tourist authority demanded to see Prime Minister Anand. 'The travel companies were clamouring for Mechai's scalp,' the former Prime Minister told me. 'They were afraid that the whole industry would collapse. They wanted Mechai removed and they said you can keep him as head of Aids, but not concurrently as head of tourism.'

The Prime Minister stood his ground and Mechai remained in charge of both tourism and Aids. Thailand's tourist industry continued to boom. 'It does prove we were correct in our assessment that it would not hurt tourism,' Mr Anand said. 'It would promote tourism.'

The key Aids initiative during the Anand regime was the adoption of a 100 per cent condom policy in the brothels. The scheme had already been piloted in the provinces, but it was now introduced right across the country. The idea was simple. All commercial sex had to be safe sex, and prostitutes were to be randomly tested for sexually transmitted diseases. If an infection was traced to a particular brothel, police had the power to close it down.

The results were remarkable. Condom use in brothels increased from 25 per cent to over 90 per cent in three years. HIV infection rates among prostitutes fell from 50 per cent in 1991 to 20 per cent a decade later. In 1991 just over 60 per cent of army conscripts were reported as using condoms in their encounters with prostitutes. Four years later the figure had risen to more than 90 per cent. In the general population, the level of sexually transmitted infections fell from more than seven cases per thousand to less than one per thousand. Senator Mechai Viravaidya had spearheaded efforts that prevented millions of infections and saved hundreds of thousands of lives.

There are those, mainly in the United States, who contest the international significance of Thailand's achievement, arguing that the lessons of massive condom availability have only limited application elsewhere. Condoms are appropriate for 'high-risk' groups like prostitutes, but they do not deserve universal promotion. Mechai emphatically rejects this view. 'What we did in Thailand was to promote condoms for everyone, not just sex workers. We said the condom is a girl's best friend.

'As for the Americans and abstinence, just give them a holiday to get over it! What has been done in Thailand has been despite the Americans not because of them. Fine, if you can manage abstinence, that's great. But you've got to have a second parachute if the first one doesn't work. You can go from abstinence to being infected or you can go from abstinence to being protected, that's all.'

Fervent international arguments over condoms intensified from 2003 with the new United States policy of promoting their use for those 'high-risk' groups but encouraging everyone else to abstain or be faithful. The US continued to be the largest supplier of condoms to the poor world, but as HIV infections multiplied the question posed by the United Nations was whether donors were doing nearly enough to bridge a growing gap between requirement and supply.

More than a billion condoms are shipped to developing countries every year, but many billions more are needed. In its 2003 report, the United Nations Population Fund referred to 'severe shortages' of condoms for family planning and disease prevention. Aid-givers might well be maintaining or even modestly increasing their supplies, but the UN said support was 'still decreasing in relative terms in relation to the increasing global need for contraceptives'. In 2005 the Commission for Africa, brainchild of Tony Blair and Bob Geldof, endorsed the extraordinary objective of a twenty-five-fold increase in condom availability in Africa.

The larger political truth was that under American influence the poor were being told that 'behaviour change' rather than condoms was the appropriate response to Aids. It was consequently unlikely that the United States would make any substantial effort to close the condom gap and so others would have to step into the breach. In recognition of a growing divide between America and Europe, the European Union referred in a statement on 1 December 2005, World Aids Day, to 'the alarming shortfall of reproductive health commodities' and added: 'We are profoundly concerned about the resurgence of partial or incomplete messages on HIV prevention which are not grounded in evidence and have limited effectiveness.' There was no reference to the United States in the document, and it has still to be seen whether Europe will convert pointed language into concrete action. The need is immediate and cannot wait on diplomatic nicety. 'In many countries people are dying because of the lack of a two cents condom,' a senior UN official told me.

Influential religious voices in the United States continue to inveigh against the culture of the condom. The Reverend Franklin Graham, son of Billy Graham, whose 'Prescription for Hope' conference in 2002 marked an important step in gaining the Bush administration's commitment to fighting global Aids, attributed the pressure for more condom supplies to godlessness on the part of the United Nations and the profit motive among manufacturers. He told me that the UN was a group of people that hated God and would not engage the Church in fighting Aids, preferring instead to work through corrupt national governments.

'Their approach is condoms. They have built their whole fight against HIV/Aids on condoms. And the condom manufacturers in England and the US have put millions into this and have profited in a huge way.'

Like many other opponents of the condom, Franklin Graham has come to the frankly improbable conclusion that Western governments and UN agencies are in the pocket of the condom companies. He told me that these manufacturers were 'buying the truth. If Aids goes away, there are a lot of people who are going to be out of money. There's a lot of money involved here – big bucks.' Graham is equally convinced that because condoms have not checked the global spread of Aids, something else has to be done. 'Since the UN about ten years ago started pushing the massive distribution of condoms around the world, the HIV infection rate has gone up, it has not gone down. That approach is failing, but they will not admit it.'

For a more measured American view on the role of condoms in the Aids crisis, I went to see Colin Powell. As President Bush's Secretary of State until the beginning of 2005, he was in formal charge of the US Aids programme for its first two years. He told me he had first learned about Aids at the Pentagon in the early 1980s when he was on the staff of Defense Secretary Caspar Weinberger and attended a briefing on the potential seriousness of this new disease for the US army. Global Aids was in his in-tray when he became Secretary of State in 2001, and he was one of those who urged President Bush to step up the American commitment. When the President said he was committing as much as $15 billion to fighting Aids, Powell was staggered. 'You want to say that again, Boss?'

Condom promotion was always an issue. Early on in the first Bush term Colin Powell got into hot water with some of the President's supporters when he was asked on an MTV youth programme about condoms, Aids and the Catholic Church. He replied that he respected the Church's view but that condoms were a way of preventing infection and 'therefore I not only support their use, I encourage their use among people who are sexually active'.

'Well, it was an interesting day, the next day,' Powell said. 'The right wing of the Republican Party rose up, the White House wanted to know, "What did he say? Get the transcript. Get the transcript." ' In fact the row was short-lived. The President did not react, the White House was supportive, and in any case Mr Powell and his family were known to be strong supporters of a well-connected Washington youth abstinence programme called 'Best Friends'. But Powell himself has not changed his mind on the importance of condoms despite Washington's emphasis since 2003 on the merits of abstinence.

Powell told me he was a great believer in ABC – Abstinence, Be Faithful and Condoms – but he never forgot any of the letters, even for young people. 'If A and B are not something that you're able to do, then protect yourself, and that's C – use condoms. I never made a distinction between young or old.'

I pointed out that the Bush Aids programme did make such a distinction. 'I didn't,' he replied. 'I never did. Maybe PEPFAR [the President's Emergency Plan for Aids Relief] does. In everything I've ever said – and I've made a lot of statements – I've never made a distinction by age with respect to ABC. My motive here is to keep these kids from getting a disease, not to keep them from moral turpitude. If they're 16 or 17 and their hormones are raging, as mine were ... I would certainly say, "You're not ready for it. OK, you can't help it. Don't start doing it with everybody, and protect yourself with condoms if you're not sure of your partner." '

I reminded him that US Christian organizations were receiving government funds for exclusive campaigns on abstinence and fidelity. 'I don't think that's the way to go about it. I think you have to have a comprehensive programme ... The argument is "If you show them how to use them then you're encouraging them, you're promoting promiscuity", as if this little piece of rubber either promotes it or doesn't promote it! That's not what causes these kids to go out and try to have a sexual relationship!'

He recalled growing up in New York City in the 1950s. 'We all walked around with condoms,' he said. 'We didn't know what the devil to do with them, but we all had one drying up in a wallet somewhere.'

Colin Powell concluded with an eloquent reference to the impact of Aids on the African American community. Black women are a staggering thirteen times more likely to become HIV-positive than their white counterparts. 'When I see some 16-year-old girl carrying the virus and she is condemned to ostracism, to stereotyping, to a life of perhaps fatal illness, and when she's carrying the risk of infecting someone else and infecting her own child, and this could have been prevented if she knew how to use a condom, or her partner did, and I'm *not* going to make her aware of that possibility? I'm sorry, that's not my approach.'

Formal religious prohibition on the use of condoms remains the biggest barrier in combating Aids. But even in the Roman Catholic Church in Africa where the hierarchy is at its most unyielding, there are humane responses from priests who have daily to confront the reality of Aids. At the huge squatter camp of Orange Farm outside Johannesburg, I spent an afternoon with Father Guido Bourgeois, a French-Canadian White Father, learning about the desperate impact of the epidemic on his parish and the fresh hope that antiretroviral treatment represents.

Father Guido told me that many families in Orange Farm were so poor that when a relative died the body often had to be kept in a municipal deep freeze for weeks before they could afford the cost of burial.

American-funded antiretrovirals had at last made people accept their sickness because they could now do something about it. 'As long as there was no treatment, no help, it was useless to declare that you had Aids,' Father Guido said. 'Now there is a small light. I always say a light is very useful during the night.'

As we sat over tea and biscuits in his sparse church house, I noticed in the corner a bold wall hanging entitled 'Fleet of Hope'. Stitched on it was one boat labelled 'Abstinence', another labelled 'Fidelity' and a rubber dinghy marked 'Condoms'. It was a game that Father Guido played with his parishioners and was aimed at encouraging them to think about how people could be saved from the waters of Aids by climbing on board one of these boats – any of the boats. The game is played with a cast of silhouette characters – a soldier, nurse, student, doctor, mine worker, taxi driver and so on – and the idea is to place each character in one or other of the boats.

Father Guido had been playing the game after Mass the previous Sunday. 'When I preach I say something different,' he told me in reference to the Church's strict views on condoms. 'This is more a social activity, a workshop on HIV/Aids. Our theme is, "Change your behaviour". If you use a condom, use it always. If you're faithful, be faithful always. If you're a kid at school, be abstinent.' How could he square any recommendation of condoms with the Church's prohibition? 'I'm not teaching in this workshop. I'm exploring the realities of life. I'm a social worker looking at life.'

He said there had been a lot of jokes last Sunday about taxi drivers. 'They are either in the deep water with HIV or they're in the small boat with the condoms.' I said to Father Guido that he had allocated quite a small boat for the condom-users. 'Yes,' he replied with a giggle, 'but it's quite full.'

The Fleet of Hope was invented by a French White Father, Bernard Joinet, who has doctorates in theology and psychology, and who arrived as a missionary in Tanzania forty years ago. He would probably still be living there had it not been for the game he invented and the rigour of the Church's view on condoms.

As chaplain and lecturer in the medical faculty at the University of Dar es Salaam, Father Bernard had been engaged in supporting people with Aids from the start of the epidemic, but he soon appreciated that the urgent need lay not in Aids care but in Aids prevention. He then told me the poetic, almost biblical story of the Fleet of Hope.

In 1994 he was leading an Aids seminar in Bukoba, in northern Tanzania, the worst affected region of the country and at that time probably the worst affected in the whole of Africa. Bukoba adjoins the Rakai district of Uganda, the epicentre of that country's own Aids epidemic. The seminar brought French medical aid workers together with Tanzanian Christians. 'We had a big fight,' said Father Bernard. 'You had the French who were advocating, "Condom! Condom! Condom!" and the Tanzanian Catholics and Lutherans who were saying, "Abstinence, faithfulness! Abstinence, faithfulness!" '

On the second day of the seminar, they broke off hostilities to visit nearby villages. In each village they found freshly dug graves in the banana plantations, and in every other house they found someone in the terminal stages of Aids. 'When I came back I blew my top,' Father Bernard continued. 'I said, "Why are we fighting each other? Nothing is working. Neither condoms nor abstinence nor faithfulness. What is the point of fighting?" '

That night Father Bernard said he had a vision. Then he quickly corrected himself, and said he had had a dream. 'I saw an expanse of water with no shore, just water, and then I saw a big boat, one of those big wooden Christopher Columbus boats, and then I woke up. Immediately I thought "Bernard, that's it." We thought that Aids was a little river and we could dam it. In fact

Aids is a flood; the water goes up and up; many people drown and those who survive in trees or on roofs lose courage because they think they will soon be caught by the waters.'

So the Fleet of Hope set sail. As an instructive game played in communities confronted by Aids, it has since been adopted by UNAIDS and used in seventy countries. For Father Bernard, the important thing is that people at risk should get out of the water and on to one of the boats – the abstinence boat, the fidelity boat or the condom boat. 'If you don't feel at ease on the boat of your choice, don't go back into the water, but change boats,' he said. It was this combination of the condom option and his respect for individual choice that put Father Bernard on a collision course with the Roman Catholic hierarchy.

On World Aids Day in 1997 Father Bernard was asked by Tanzanian officials if he would go on national television and demonstrate his Fleet of Hope. He dutifully sought permission from the head of the Church in Tanzania, Cardinal Polycarp Pengo, Archbishop of Dar es Salaam. 'Yes, Father, you can go,' said the Cardinal, 'but you can only go with two of the boats.' Father Bernard did not go.

In 1998 he received a letter from the Catholic bishops of Tanzania complaining that his Fleet of Hope ignored the teachings of the Church and informing him that he was to be dismissed with immediate effect from his posts of chaplain and lecturer at the university. His students protested, and a compromise was reached that he would retire on his seventieth birthday in 1999. Father Bernard then returned to France after more than thirty years of service in Tanzania. Happily he still visits the country and his advice is still sought elsewhere in Africa.

Father Bernard's enforced retirement was not his last clash with Cardinal Pengo. At an international Aids conference in Tanzania in 2002, the Fleet of Hope figured in a discussion on condoms initiated by another priest out of step with the Catholic hierarchy. The Cardinal was asked to comment, and he denounced them both on local television as 'traitors to the priesthood'. 'It hurt me,' said Father Bernard, 'but I live with it.'

He went on: 'I have a conviction. It is very simply that you have to preach the whole gospel.' Of the commandments of God there are three which he singles out: 'One, that you shall not fornicate. Secondly, you should be faithful. But the sixth commandment is that you should not kill. I have to insist on "You shall not kill", but no one preaches that in church.'

Making Aids History

Esther Kamusa, the 37-year-old Zambian woman with whom I began this book, did not have to die. Neither did her daughter have to be left an Aids orphan. Of the 25 million who have died since 1981, many could have been saved. They died because governments, in the rich world and the poor world, and institutions with global responsibility like the churches failed in their humanitarian duty.

Will any good come from the Aids catastrophe? Will there be any worthwhile memorial to those who have died and will still die? It is not easy to see light in this darkness, but Aids has clearly illuminated the depth of Africa's development crisis and offers some new starting-points.

In the fields of health and education, the crisis has underlined the consequences of decline and the need for rebuilding. Without functioning health systems, Aids will never be tackled, let alone reversed, and without better education, boys and girls will not grow up to deal with all the social challenges presented by the epidemic. Governments in the poor world must make an earnest priority of health and education, and the rich world must never again put demands for fiscal discipline ahead of people's lives.

Esther suffered because she was a woman. Most of the people newly infected with HIV in Africa are women. They have little or no control over their sexual and reproductive lives. They are often coerced into sex and cannot insist on protection. In the rich world, one of their most eloquent spokeswomen is Sandy Thurman, formerly President Clinton's senior Aids official.

'I don't give a damn how many billions of dollars we dump into this epidemic,' she says. 'If we don't change these social norms, we will fail.' Is she optimistic? 'I have firmly believed for the past eight years that the silver lining to this cloud will be a fundamental shift in the way we look at women's issues.'

Esther Kamusa's life could also have been saved with drugs that have been available for the past decade in the rich world. Only with the Bush administration's commitment to Aids relief has there been any real prospect of poor HIV-positive people in poor countries receiving the treatment they need.

The Bush plan set a concrete target of putting 2 million on antiretroviral drugs by 2008. Then, during Tony Blair's 'Year of Africa', the G8 countries extended this commitment 'with the aim' of reaching 'as close as possible to universal access to treatment for all those who need it by 2010'. That amounts to a promise to HIV-positive people in Africa, who must not be fobbed off with the careful equivocations of summit communiqués.

The breakthrough on medical treatment for HIV-positive people in the poor world only happened because organizations such as Médecins Sans Frontières and Treatment Action Campaign in South Africa took on the big pharmaceutical companies. Big Pharma's world changed with the collapse of its case against the South African government in 2001, and here again Aids must become the agent of sustained and radical change.

The rich world has now recognized that all people with HIV, however poor, have a right to life, and the same principle must be applied to other diseases. Here there are also signs of hope. Thanks to alliances between pharmaceutical companies, big philanthropic organizations and rich governments, new research is under way on malaria and tuberculosis, and other neglected tropical diseases are beginning to receive proper attention.

Concentrating on HIV treatment has had the effect of pushing Aids prevention to the sidelines, which is where many governments have been happy to keep it. In the early years it did not require large sums of money or interventions of great sophistication to tackle the epidemic. Often it needed a simple determination to treat Aids as a public health problem, not a moral commentary, to tell people openly and clearly how to prevent infection and to provide them with the means of doing so.

That did not happen because Aids raises moral and sexual issues that have consistently clouded the judgement of politicians and undermined their ability to act in the public interest. What began as a common prejudice against gays in the 1980s has mutated into objections to other lifestyles and practices, providing public officials with more excuses for failing to carry out their public health duties.

As the twenty-fifth anniversary of the epidemic approached, the United States chose to embark on an international moral crusade in the name of Aids prevention. Instead of promoting condoms as an essential defence for young people and the population at large, it promotes abstinence and fidelity. Instead of minimizing the health risks faced by intravenous drug users, it maintains a scientifically unmerited ban on needle exchange programmes. Instead of working with prostitutes' rights organizations to make sure these women stay healthy and do not spread HIV, it demands that prostitution be denounced.

The Bush administration's vision in 2003 was to 'turn the tide of this global pandemic' and it has set a target of preventing 7 million HIV infections by 2008. It has committed impressive resources to that end, but it has hedged its commitment with the agenda of the self-righteous Right. A 'Just Say No' approach characterized the US government's initial response to Aids in the 1980s, with severe consequences for the spread of the epidemic. Twenty-five years into this global catastrophe it is adding more deaths to the Aids body count.

Further Reading

The classic early Aids book is Randy Shilts, *And the Band Played On* (St Martin's Press, New York, 1987), a detailed and compelling account of the initial US failure to deal with the epidemic. Shilts was a gay reporter on the *San Francisco Chronicle* and died of Aids in 1994.

Larry Kramer, quoted in the first chapter of this book, compiled *Reports from the Holocaust: The Story of an Aids Activist* (St Martin's Press, New York, 1994) from his furious and brilliant writing on the US response to Aids.

A measured analysis and a powerful personal account of the anguish created by South Africa's Aids 'denialism' is Edwin Cameron, *Witness to Aids* (Tafelberg Publishers, Cape Town, 2005). Judge Cameron is the most prominent South African publicly to acknowledge his HIV-positive status.

Two South African journalists have devoted strong chapters to Aids in their books on the new South Africa. They are Allister Sparks, *Beyond the Miracle* (Jonathan Ball Publishers, South Africa, and Profile Books, London, 2003) and William Mervin Gumede, *Thabo Mbeki and the Battle for the Soul of the ANC* (Zebra Press, Cape Town, 2005).

The most important book on the early British epidemic is Virgina Berridge, *Aids in the UK – The Making of Policy,* 1981-1994 (Oxford University Press, Oxford, 1996). Dr Berridge shows how sound public health principles overcame conservatism and prejudice at the height of the Thatcher era.

There is a valuable narrative of the US response to global Aids, notably during the Clinton years, in Greg Behrman, *The Invisible People* (Free Press, New York, 2004). Esther Kaplan, *With God on Their Side* (The New Press, New York, 2004), provides critical detail on the influence of the religious Right in the era of George W. Bush and has a chapter entitled 'Aids, Born Again'.

The most influential contemporary book on global Aids is Edward C. Green, *Rethinking Aids Prevention* (Praeger, Westport, Ct., 2003), which played a decisive role in gaining official US endorsement for Uganda's ABC approach to prevention, favouring A (Abstinence) and B (Be Faithful) over C (Condoms).

Readers interested in the new US approach should start with *The President's Emergency Plan for Aids Relief*, published in 2003 and available at www.stategov/documents/organization/29831.pdf. It is a readable and clear-cut exposition of America's determination to overturn decades of public-health consensus in the fields of sexual health and Aids.

A valuable counterpoint to the claims and ambitions of governments in the field of Aids can be found in a series of superb reports from Human Rights Watch in New York. They are available in the HIV/Aids section under Global Issues at their website www.hrw.org.

Acknowledgements

My big debt is to former colleagues at the BBC World Service Trust. Roy Head, then its health director, sent me to India in 1999 to run a leprosy campaign and encouraged me to stay on to run an HIV/Aids campaign. Neither would have succeeded without the skills and commitment of Lori McDougall who managed both projects. My colleagues in Delhi were a delight to work with. I single out Saloni Puri, now the project's managing editor, with whom I shared an office and who accompanied me on visits to Indian officials where we were told that some of our anti-HIV media messages were unacceptable because they promoted condoms and would be taken off the air. That experience introduced me to the politics of Aids and the perverse response of some politicians to the epidemic. It was also the genesis of this book. The government which banned our material was defeated in 2004, and replaced by one more open-minded in its efforts to combat Aids.

During my travels, I received much help and hospitality from friends. I would like to thank George and Chrissie Griffin with whom I stayed in Washington, and Bob and Ompie Liebenthal with whom I stayed in Lusaka. In Brazil I would not have been able to meet so many remarkable people without the assistance of Eliane Gonçalves Izolan, a deeply committed journalist in the field of Aids and now a friend. I am also grateful to Giselle Portenier, who ran the BBC World Service Trust project in Cambodia, for her hospitality in Phnom Penh and for organizing valuable interviews.

I had the good fortune to find Profile as my publisher because of the interest and advice of Justine Hardy. She introduced me to Gail Pirkis who stuck with the idea behind this book and with whom it has been a pleasure to work.

Aids officials, researchers and activists around the world were generous with information and contacts. Some would prefer not to be thanked in public. Among those who may not mind are: Alvaro Bermejo and Mandeep Dhaliwal of the International HIV/Aids Alliance; Jo Ford, now of the Commonwealth Secretariat; Anton Kerr; Tom Lawson of NAM; Sharonann Lynch of Health GAP; Rebecca Schleifer of Human Rights Watch; Ann Smith of Cafod; Lyndall Stein of Concern; and Wendy Turnbull of Population Action International.

A number of knowledgeable people helped me review the text and made valuable comments. They were Joe Amon at Human Rights Watch; Roy Head, now running Development Media International; Bill Johnson; Bob Liebenthal; Jamie Love at CPTech; Lori McDougall; Lisa Power at the Terrence Higgins Trust; and Gerry Stimson at the International Harm Reduction Association. My great friend Ned Campbell cast a beaky schoolmaster's eye over my English. No one but me is responsible for the remaining errors of fact and judgement.

Peter Gill
December 2005

Index

Z